06/25/05

Candace,

Thank you for the ongoing friendship & support. Enjoy the trip down memory lane.

MW01610129

About the Author

Daniel T. Bloom SCRP – Daniel Bloom has over twenty-five years of experience in the relocation industry having started by completing Ben Franklin closes on destination locations for candidates he recruited as an executive headhunter. During his career he has been an appraiser, a member of the internal human resources staff of a Fortune 1000 corporation and a licensed real estate professional including the development of relocation departments within several real estate broker firms in the Tampa Bay area of Florida. He holds a Bachelor's Degree in Education from Parsons College in Fairfield, Iowa.

More Praise for
Just Get Me There:

"This book is absolutely one of its kind. What an outstanding reference for the relocation industry. Your detailed research heralds the past hero architects of the industry, examines the present state of our industry and clearly outlines what is needed to survive the future. This will be truly a must read for anyone who wants to be considered a relocation professional. Congratulations! A herculean task well done!"

Laura Herring
President
Impact Group St. Louis, MO

"I have finished your wonderful – absolutely wonderful – book. You really must be complimented on the research you have done…If this does not become a text book for anyone who enters the Relocation Industry I will be surprised, this is an assembly of details which should be mandatory for anyone who enters this field.

"CONGRATULATIONS – FANTASTIC – thanks for sharing."

Marita Bruun
Former President Lifeco Relocation
Former Vice President Texas National Bank Relocation

Just Get Me There

A Journey Through Corporate
Relocation

Daniel T. Bloom SCRP

Gom Paraclete Press

An imprint of Gom Publishing, LLC
P.O. Box 211110, Columbus, Ohio 43221

Phone: 866.466.2608
Email: communications@gompublishing.com
Internet: **www.gompublishing.com**

Copyright © 2005 by Daniel Bloom & Associates, Inc.

All rights reserved. No part of this book may be used or reproduced in any manner whatsoever without written permission, except in the case of brief quotations embodied in critical articles and reviews. For information address Gom Paraclete Press, an division of Gom Publishing, LLC.

The views presented in this book are not necessarily those of the Publisher.

Library of Congress Cataloging-in-Publication Data

Bloom, Daniel T.
  Just get me there : a journey through corporate relocation / by Daniel T. Bloom.
     p. cm.
  ISBN 1-932966-34-x (hardback : acid-free paper) -
  ISBN 1-932966-08-0 (pbk. : acid-free paper)
   1. Employees--Relocation--United States--History. 2. Business relocation--United States--History. 3. Storage and moving trade--United States--History. I. Title.
  HF5549.5.R47B56 2003
  658.3'83--dc22
                                    2005010106

First Gom Paraclete Press printing: May 2005

1 3 5 7 9 10 8 6 4 2

Cover design by Stephen Fox and Justin May

Table of Contents

INTRODUCTION

If we look at virtually every civilization in recorded history, each has had an elder in place of authority whose primary responsibility was to pass on the knowledge and history of that society on to the succeeding generations. The position of elder within the societal structure was one of reverence. Younger members of the society would listen with great respect to these knowledge bearers. As we have become more modernized, the role of elder has diminished or disappeared altogether. The relocation industry has had no such elder interaction. Unfortunately, the elders of our industry have started the exodus to other endeavors whether that is retirement or into other fields altogether such as teaching or human relations. The difficulty here is that the elders of our industry have not taken the necessary steps to pass down the knowledge to their replacements. The relocation professional of today has no clue as to where the industry came from. The result is that the replacements know what the industry expects of them but have little or no idea as to what went on in this industry from the 1950's up until the present. They know what an amended value transaction is for example, but do not understand the reasoning behind using that transaction instead of an assigned sale transaction. They have no idea what the early pioneers went through in order to create an industry, which now pays the modern relocation professional's salary. This is not an anomaly. If recent polls are any indication, many of us watch the Tonight Show with Jay Leno on a fairly regular basis. One of the ongoing segments of the show is called *Jay Walking*. For those of you who have never have watched the segment, Jay Leno goes out on the streets of Los Angeles and asks a series of questions pertaining to a topic, which should be of common knowledge to the participants. Like many of you, I have watched these segments and have laughed at the seemingly ridiculous answers to those simple questions. However, if we look at the responses from another perspective they are an example of how we have forgotten the historical roots of the relocation industry. Bruce Cole, Chairman of the National Endowment for the Humanities, calls this lack of knowledge *American amnesia*. It is not just Jay Walking; many polls have indicated that we as a civilization are losing any concept of past events in our historical time line. Our governmental officials tell us that unless something is over a century old it has no place in our daily environment. Relocation is at best half of that in tenure.

In 1973, while working as an executive recruiter, a candidate I had just placed posed a rather formidable question. He asked for a comparison

The term American Amnesia was presented as part of an address called "The Urgency of Memory." It was part of the program called "Art in an age of Uncertainty," organized by New York University and presented June 7, 2002 in New York City. The full excerpt of the address can be found on Wall Street Journal Online dated June 11, 2002.

between the community in which he currently resided and the community I was moving him to. This was my initial exposure to the industry I have called home for the past thirty years.

In an article, which I wrote and which was recently published in *Mobility* magazine (August 2002), I looked at the issue of "Where have all the Elders Gone?" Recognizing that things change as we are told in Ecclesiastes, "For everything there is a season, and a time for every purpose..." I want to make it clear that we as relocation professionals are not against change. But that change needs to be rooted in the historical basis of our knowledge and our traditions.... As an offshoot of the *Mobility* article mentioned above, several people made the comment that what was sorely needed within the industry was a solid reference that would provide this historical basis to all within the industry. To the new relocation professional, this reference would provide a guide through the development of the industry, why we do what we do, and why certain policies have evolved in the direction they have. For the still-active and retired elders of the industry still active within the industry, this would provide a trip down memory lane. The goal of the work you are about to read is to pass on the elder's knowledge to succeeding generations of relocation professionals. This is not to say that no knowledge has been passed on. The exceptions to such a blanket statement can be found in the appendix entitled *Circle Unbroken* which shows the reader the offspring of the early pioneers who have followed in their parents' footsteps and have molded a career for themselves within this industry. During the course of the research for this book, I have identified over two hundred individuals who have played a role in the growth of this industry. Through interviews with many of them, I have been guided in providing the reader with a feel for where the relocation industry has come from and in what direction we are headed. I want to thank the individuals who have assisted in the development of the resource list; Cris Collie who has led the Employee Relocation Council for most of its history, David DuMez (3M, Relocation Resources); Harvey Auger (Homequity); Mickey Williams (Associates Relocation, US Relocation, Capital Relocation); Liam Murphy of the Relocation Business News and George Leddicotte (Feasibility Group); Terry Needham formerly the Editor of the Relocation Update for sending me a copy of his book *Winning and Keeping Relocation Business*. I truly appreciate the efforts of those who have retired from this industry but still are willing to discuss the path they took as this industry developed. Many of these elders I have talked with were very happy that this was finally being put in documented form. Unfortunately, some of the pioneers had passed away prior starting this project. Further, I am also appreciative of the current members of the profession who were equally willing to share their knowledge of modern relocation. I need to make particular mention of individuals in and outside the industry who have also been of great assistance by taking time out of their busy schedules to talk with us about the past and future of the relocation industry such as Andy Anderson, the corporate historian for Wells Fargo Company, for the details about the early relocations of his employer; Marita Bruun, Texas Commerce Bank; Dr. Weston Edwards Ph.D.; Dick Farance; Darlene Firestone; Charles Gardiner; Laura Herring; Meri Hill; John Huggins; Greg Hutchins; James Keane; John Kovach; Derek Lewin; John Lotty; C. Marvin Mandery; Lisa Milovanic; John Moore; Frank Patitucci; Charles Peterson; Bob Quietmeyer; Sam Raguso; Ken Rich; Doug Shepard; Art Stoddard; Bruce Walczak; Mickey Williams and Joan Madden. I also would like to thank Candace Fitzpatrick with help on the development of the American Telephone and Telegraph case study; Linda Gross at the Hagley Museum and Library for her help in locating summaries of some of the early research reports into the industry, Amey Hutchins at the Wharton School for information on the 1960 thesis done on the relocation industry, Robin Merker who has held a very special place in my life for over twenty-five years and who proofread the final manuscript, and her husband, Michael Merker who read the manuscript for its flow and presentation. In a project this large it is critical to make sure that our data is correct and we thank Harvey Auger and Mickey Williams who checked the manuscript for its accuracy. I need to also thank my wife Cheryl and two sons Joel and Joshua for putting up with me during this process.

Part I

The Journey Begins

If you were to ask almost anyone who has some knowledge of the relocation industry as to when it all started, most will provide you with a date somewhere in the late 1950's or early sixties. While we agree that most of the developmental changes within the relocation industry took place during a fifty year time span from 1953 to the present, we can not look at the history of the industry without going back further in time.

Based on our research, the first individuals who could rightly call themselves corporate transferees took place in 1852. According to the book *Stagecoach* by Philip L, Fradkin and Andy Anderson, Wells Fargo and Company decided to open an office in San Francisco at the beginning of the gold rush. The company asked Samuel P. Carter, who was an express and telegraph agent in Albany, New York and Reuben W. Washburn who was a banker from Syracuse, New York, to open the office. Unlike the relocations of today, they headed to the West Coast by steamship via either the end of South America or across the Panama Isthmus by canoe and kayak. The length of the trip was approximately fifty-one days, rather than less than a week, and carried a number of hazards the least of which was malaria and other tropical menaces. In a copy of a letter provided by Wells Fargo, Samuel Carter wrote on June 30, 1852 to the corporate offices, "If my health was only good I should feel in good spirits. I am improving & they tell me I will soon get strength & flesh – I am 21 lbs lighter than when I left N.Y. think I shall be right in a few days."

At the time of the move, Wells Fargo and American Express were owned by the same parent organization.

With a great deal more research, we could further report the challenges of relocating in those times as compared to today. However, in the time period from 1852 until the 1950's, there were very little in the way of events within the industry, so we will concentrate our review of the history of the industry on the last fifty years. Our review of the history begins with a look at who the founders were, where did they come from, and what their vision was.

1

THE
FOUNDERS
OF
THE
INDUSTRY
AND
THEIR
VISION

T he modern relocation industry began in the early 1950's as a solution to a business need. At that time, many of the larger financial institutions created *trust departments*. Their purpose was to handle the large monetary transactions of their corporate clients. Among these corporate clients were International Business Machines and Exxon Oil, who made the business decision to ask theses trust departments to handle the funding of the equity on the homes of their corporate transferees. These two corporations set up an informal network of over fifty banks trust departments across the country to handle the business. While it could have been the start of a formal process, the trust departments were not set up to work as a network, and each of the financial institutions operated totally independent of the other banks in the system. There were still other professionals who also saw the need for these types of services and became actively involved in the growth and development of the relocation industry.

In 1955, Don McPherson is credited with the beginnings of this industry with the start of Homerica.

The question before us becomes, Where did the early pioneers come from and what attracted them to relocation? The answer to this depends on what segment of the industry you are looking at. Each segment had its own reasons for entering the field. Let's look at those segments and who they represented.

Corporate America

Corporate America was beginning to deal with a mobile society and the family became more involved in the relocation process. The result was that the personnel departments began to look for ways to assist their employees with the move. Further, the movement of household goods required the assistance from the *traffic departments*. These were departments that were created by corporations to deal with the logistics of the movement of materials from corporate location to corporate location. So when the corporation entered the picture with relocation assistance, it was natural for the traffic department to coordinate the movement of household goods for the employee. Still another player in the process was the financial end of the corporation. If the corporation decided to become involved in the sale of the employee's home, the financial aspects were often handled by the *real estate department* which was part of the treasury department of the corporation. Many of the early corporate pioneers were discussing the issue of relocation and its impact on the corporation at various American Management Association sponsored seminars held across the country. It was often the personnel responsible for the relocation program who attended these seminars.

Service Side

The service side of the picture saw the push for the development of relocation services coming from several sources. Among these early views was a thesis done at the Wharton School of Business that looked at the potential for such a successful enterprise. The preparer of the thesis went out and talked to over fifty corporations regarding their relocation needs and their openness to using a service to assist them. One outcome of this study was the creation of the American Relocation Service by John Huggins as will be discussed in Chapter 3. Other individuals got into the business by virtue of their running successful real estate organizations, which assisted transferees who were visiting their communities.

Out of both these groups, several individuals seemed to make their presence known more than others.

Ted Bell

Ted Bell was a Chicago area real estate broker who, through a subsidiary company, developed a program which guaranteed the sale of a prior residence of a purchaser of a new home if it did not sell in a certain period of time. Later, he went to work for Chicago Title, which led him to the formation of the Employee Transfer Corporation.

Weston Edwards

Weston Edwards graduated from Harvard Business School with a Doctorate in Business Administration and went to work for Donaldson, Lufkin, and Jennerette. While working there he did a review of the relocation industry and saw the potential for further business expansion. Shortly afterwards he left the investment banking industry to join this new developing industry.

Charles Gardiner

Charles Gardiner was a graduate of the Naval Academy and a Barker Scholar during his further studies at Harvard Business School. Following his graduation from Harvard, he joined Transamerica Insurance and rose to the position of Executive Vice President of Financial and Strategic Planning. When Transamerica made the decision to enter the relocation field he was asked to head up the effort.

Dan Hanrahan

Dan Hanrahan was a New Jersey real estate broker who had ties to the Howard Savings Bank. He created the very first third-party company called *Potere*.

John Kovach

John Kovach attended the University of Missouri. While a student, he took some vocational testing at the University's career center. The results of the testing indicated that he should go into real estate. At the time the Dean of the Business School was a local real estate agent who encouraged John to try his had at residential real estate. He tried residential real estate for a short time but much preferred the arena of corporate real estate. Kovach was one of the first five graduates of the real estate department at the University of Missouri. He then went to work in the real estate department of the Bank of St. Louis. The Bank had a pocket venture to handle the relocations for Southwestern Bell, and John was selected to take the next six months to put the program together. From the time of his graduation, he was seeking real estate – not relocation. He felt that if corporate real estate did not work out he could always go elsewhere.

Derek Lewin

Derek Lewin graduated from the University of Colorado with a major in history and a minor in economics. Following graduation Mr. Lewin went to work for Hertz Rent-a-Car, eventually becoming the youngest manger being given responsibility for the mountain region for the company. During his stint with Hertz, he had the opportunity to meet with Don McPherson. This meeting became the entry for Mr. Lewin into the relocation industry with Homequity and later the first asset management firm in the country.

Frank Madden

Frank Madden attended Georgetown University on his benefits under the GI Bill and finished his college education in two years. From there he went on to Georgetown Law School earning his law degree. After one year of law school, he joined the Federal Bureau of Investigation as an agent for a number of years. Following his stint with the Bureau, he tried his hand at running a legal practice, which was not to his liking. He then joined Union Carbide in their real estate department. He remained there until joining Homequity in the early 1960's.

C. Marvin Mandery

C. Marvin Mandery began his career in 1951 in the human resource department of General Mills. His first exposure to relocation was dealing with new hire relocations in which the policy was designed by each division of the company. Later in the 1950's he became responsible for college recruiting as an adjunct to relocation. He attended a number of the American Management Association seminars dealing with relocation issues. For the next twenty years, the relocation program reported directly to him at General Mills.

Don McPherson

Don McPherson was a college book editor for McGraw Hill based in Chicago. He was a Ph.D graduate of Harvard. McPherson entered into an agreement with a prospective partner to open a publishing company based in New York City.

Charles Peterson

Charles Peterson is a graduate of the University of Pennsylvania's Wharton School of Business. Following his graduation he joined the Byron Reed Company in the Property Management Division and later in the Syndication Department. When one of their clients asked the company to assist with the relocation of some new employees, he entered the relocation industry.

Relocation University

While not an actual founder of the industry, in the early to mid 1960's, many of their business graduates became active in the industry through the efforts of James Keane and others at Homequity. The center of their efforts was a Jesuit institution of higher education known as *Fairfield University*. Even in the current state of the industry, there are still Fairfield University graduates in the upper levels of management of some of the relocation management firms.

The Vision

In talking with many of the elders of our industry, the general thought was that the early pioneers of this industry had no vision as to where this industry would be in the new millennium. They were basically service providers who saw a need required by the business entities and filled that need. The need was to assist the relocating family to get moved to the new location – pure and simple. The primary focus of the service delivery model was on the destination side rather than the departure side of the move. Some of the early pioneers may have felt that there was the possibility of a synergy among the various aspects of the process, but none foresaw the industry as it is fifty years later. In fact, Don McPherson never thought that the volume within the industry would ever exceed five hundred transfers a year!

2

1950
~
1959

The fifties decade was a period of great transition in the workforce. The primary workforce as the fifties began was comprised of members of what Lynne Lancaster and David Stillman, in their book *When Generations Collide,* refer to as the *Traditionalists.* These workers were born between 1900 and 1946. This group felt that if they were asked to move for their company, they had no choice but to accept the transfer for the good of their career. Tie this with the returning G.I.'s from the war to end all wars – World War II. Prior to Congress passing the G.I. Bill in 1944, it was common for an individual to be born and go through his lifetime without moving more than ten miles from his place of birth. With the passage of the G.I. Bill, the low interest loans, vocational training and other benefits under the law, there no longer was any reason to continue this trend. For the first time in our history, we became a highly mobile workforce. The Unites States Census Bureau reports that during the ten years from 1950-1959, over fifty million citizens of this country moved from one state to another which was previously unheard of. This change is significant when the data shows that in 1950, the population of this country was only one hundred fifty million people. This means that a little over a third of the population moved during this decade.

As with any new endeavor, the beginnings of this industry were very meager on events. At the very beginning of the decade, an organization known as *Fantus* began in the Midwest. Fantus was one of the first organizations to assist corporations in making sophisticated bottom-line decisions about moving corporate headquarters to new locations, and this created the relocation of employees as part of this mobile society in which we found ourselves in. In 1951, Congress authorized the creation of a system of deferring capital gains on the sale of real estate to a later date in time. Prior to this, when a homeowner sold their home, they were expected to pay the taxes that were due on the gains that were achieved as home prices increased. Under the new legislation homeowners were able to hold those taxes until a later date, usually at the time of retirement, and then pay the taxes. This system allowed the transferee to have more funds available for the down payment on that new home. This was helpful because by 1955 the median price of homes in the country had reached $13,400.

Advent of the Moving Brokerage Industry

With the dawn of the mobile workforce, the transferring family needed

The official name was the Servicemen's Readjustment Act of 1944 which initiated the education and employment benefits for returning soldiers. It also provided low interest mortgages for soldiers who wanted to buy a home upon their return.

As reported in the Annual Geographical Mobility Rates, By Type of Movement 1947-2001.

When the Household Goods Industry was deregulated, the Surface Transportation Board replaced the Interstate Commerce Commission. Both organizations were responsible for setting the tariffs, which the moving companies use to charge their customers.

to get its personal effects to the new location. Typically, this meant they would contact a household goods mover and arrange the move. For discussion's sake, let's assume that the family was moving from New York to Nebraska. The family would contact the mover in New York, who would provide the family with an estimate and, once accepted, would move the family. The caveat here was that in order to complete the move to Omaha, the movers needed to receive authority from the Interstate Commerce Commission to be able to operate in Nebraska. In order to try and relieve some of these conditions, the Interstate Commerce Commission issued authority to six moving companies to act as moving brokers. This issuance allowed these companies to go beyond the individual authority given to specific moving companies and use any van line company anywhere in the United States. The deciding factor was whether the chosen van line had both the capacity and the truck availability to handle the move when the transferee needed to move.

There were several advantages to this new system. One advantage was that the broker did not have to spend an enormous amount of money on equipment. Instead of using their own trucks, the brokers could utilize the equipment of the various movers contracted to make the move. Another advantage was that the brokers had no restriction on their operating abilities. Due to the authority terms given to the van lines, most of the moving companies remained regionally based. Now they could go anywhere. Part of the broker program was that each customer was supplied with a moving card with a number where they could reach someone if they had a problem, twenty -four hours a day, seven days a week. The final advantage was that the broker had total control of the shipment. The moving broker received part of the fee charged by the household goods company to the transferee, which funded the process. This did not cost the van line any additional cost as the brokerage fee was built into the tariffs established by the Interstate Commerce Commission. With the evolution of the brokerage concept, the groundwork was laid for many of the third-party relocation companies to eventually become moving brokers.

Early Tax Implications

We also saw the Internal Revenue Service begin to impose its views on the relocation process. In 1954, the Internal Revenue Service issued a series of Published Revenue Rulings. The first was Revenue Ruling 54-429 (1954-2 C.B. 53) in which the issue before the Internal Revenue Service was whether when an employee – in this case an Army officer – is transferred in the interest of his employer from one official station to another for permanent duty, is the allowance or reimbursement received for moving himself, his immediate family, household goods, and personal effects part of his taxable income. In the case under review, the question was whether the amounts received by an employee were to be treated as income for the preparation of income tax returns. The Internal Revenue Service stated that since the costs of moving the employee were for the benefit of the employer, the reimbursement was not compensatory in nature and, therefore, did not need to be included as income. The Internal Revenue Service did, however, state that any excess of expense over the reimbursement would be part of the employee's gross income. The ruling also went on to say that any moving expenses paid or incurred by the employee in excess of the allowances or reimbursements are not deductible for Federal income tax purposes. The ruling further stated that in any case where the transfer is made primarily for the benefit of the employee, any allowance or reimbursement received by the employee is included in his gross income .The final segment of this ruling stated that allowances for meals and lodging for the employee and family while awaiting permanent quarters at the new post of duty are also includible as gross income to the employee. In 1955, the Internal Revenue Service issued an additional ruling, Revenue Ruling 55-140 (1955-1 C.B. 317), which stated that under the Tax Code section 24(a) of 1939 Internal Revenue Act allowances for moving expenses were not an allowable tax deduction. At the end of the decade, the Internal Revenue Service issued two additional rulings that would lay the groundwork for relocation tax issues in the future. The first decision was Revenue Ruling 59-236 (1959-2 C.B. 234) in which a corporate taxpayer with headquarters in New York hired a new employee living in California. In accordance with its relocation policy, the corporate taxpayer agreed to pay a fixed rate mileage allowance to the employee to cover the cost of travel by automobile from the employee's former residence to the headquarters location of the taxpayer. The ruling by the Internal Revenue Service was that the amounts paid by an employer to or on behalf of a newly hired employee for the expenses incurred by such employee in moving to the new place of employment are, under the circumstances, "wages" for Federal employment tax purposes and for the purpose of the withholding of income tax at source on wages. Part of their evidence for the ruling was the findings in Revenue Ruling 55-140, mentioned above.

The IRS issues three types of opinions dealing with tax issues. A *Published Revenue Ruling* is an opinion that details the issues and findings behind a particular issue and can be used as a precedent for all tax payers. The second type of opinion is called a *Private Letter Ruling.* It is an opinion provided to a particular taxpayer and is for the use of that taxpayer although it provides a view of the thinking of the IRS on that issue. The final type of opinion is issued when a field agent asks for assistance on a tax matter that the field agent requests information from the national tax office. This final type of opinion is called a *Technical Advise Memorandum.*

The Internal Revenue Service followed this with Revenue Ruling 59-410 (1959-2 C.B. 64), which discussed the question of whether the charging of travel and other business expenses to an employer through the use of credit cards or other means constituted an accounting by the employee for such expenses under the accountability standards for reporting relocation expenses to an employer. The corporate taxpayer in this case stated that they furnish credit cards to its employees for the purpose of having charged directly to the corporation all the reasonable and necessary travel and entertainment expenses incurred by its employees in connection with their employment. The ruling stated that the charging of traveling and other business expenses to a corporate credit card did not constitute an accounting to an employer for the expenses. Therefore, it did not meet the accountability rule standards. These standards are still in existence today and apply for the accounting of relocation expenses on company paid relocation reimbursement expenses.

Research into the Industry Capabilities

As corporations began to become interested in the various aspects of moving their employees, the business community issued several research reports on the topic. In 1954, the American Management Association issued a report entitled *Corporate Practices in Employee Transfers*. According to all the available sources reviewed, this was the first in-depth review of the relocation industry ever completed. Conducted by Judith Calver, a research assistant on the staff of the American Management Association, her findings were based on a possible survey population of ninety-four firms of which fifty-five returned the survey forms. Ms. Calver made the statement that one of the reasons for the lack of response was that possibly there was a lack of formal personnel practices involved with relocation. Most elders who are still available indicated that this was a true picture of the early days of the industry. Conducted in the spring of 1954, the survey was designed to determine the current practices at the time in both individual transfers and relocation.

In talking to the leading long-distance movers, the American Management Association learned that the single largest customer group in 1954 were the employees who were being transferred by their employers. These relocations were created out of several events occurring in corporate America. First, the highly mobile workforce created vacancies in corporate facilities across the country. As the vacancies were created, control decisions were shifted from corporate headquarters (centralized decision making) to the divisional level (decentralized decision making). Second, the highly mobile workforce enabled corporations to reassess the need to remain in one location forever. So the work of organizations like Fantus began, and with their assistance corporations relocated whole departments, divisions, or the company entirely to new locations for any number of valid reasons.

The final reason that corporations were relocating employees was the origination of the belief that asking an employee to relocate to another division or department was to aid the employee in developing their career ladder towards management within the company. This movement also taught the corporations that the relocation benefit package could make the difference between a successful relocation and a failure. The beginning of the relocation process was the development of a program to provide moving allowances to certain critically needed employees. If we compare this effort to modern relocation policies, the system had begun with the creation of the payment of lump sum amounts to cover necessary expenses. As has been the norm over this journey, those firms who had some experience in moving employees were more generous in what they provided than firms that were relatively brand new to the process.

The second study followed two years later in 1956. Entitled *Company Payment of Employees' Moving Expenses*, the results of this study were published in the Conference Board's Highlights for the Executive, Studies in Personnel Policy, No. 154. The study looked at three types of corporate relocation.

151 companies that initiated only occasional transfers comprised the first group. The Conference Board found that these companies were willing to pay the moving expenses for several reasons. The primary reasons were a) to induce employees to willingly to become part of the mobile workforce, and; b) to facilitate executive development as was found in the earlier American Management Association study.

This also was the first time that corporations openly stated that one of their intentions was to protect employees from suffering a loss as a result of the move. The industry began to refer to this as a *womb-to-tomb* culture. The goal was to make sure the employee was kept whole as far as costs were concerned. For the first time, relocation became an employee benefit rather than a real estate program. This came about as corporations took moving expenses out of the wage and salary spectrum.

This was the beginning of what some relocation professionals referred to as the *relocation benefit corporate culture*. The first type described here was called *womb-to-tomb* in which the management of the corporation was willing to do whatever was necessary to make the employee whole as far as relocation expenses were concerned. The second cultural environment was called *cost conscious*. In this scenario, the corporate management was willing to do what ever it could to assist the transferee with relocation costs but within a prescribed financial scope. The final type of relocation cultural is called *rough justice*. In this scenario, the corporation tells the employee that it will provide a set amount towards the cost of the relocation and anything extra is their responsibility.

Finally as the benefits unfurled, the ultimate goal was to maintain both employee morale and the productivity level. As the Conference Board reviewed existing policies, it became apparent that for the first time the benefits were scaled depending on the employee's level within the company. Practically all of the firms that responded to the Conference Board paid the expenses for their most senior employees. This trend is still evident fifty-plus years later in the 21st Century. If we look at the relocation packages described in the responses, the relocation assistance packages consisted of home finding trips for both the employee and the spouse; rental losses; rental assistance; assistance in disposing of the old residence; loss on sale; purchase loans; and covering the expenses of the final trip. As now, most corporations covered the cost of moving the personal effects of the employee to the new location and possibly paying for some storage in transit. They also reported covering temporary living expenses and return trips if the employee had to report before the family could join him.

The second group consisted of thirty companies who based relocation on a tactical decision to relocate corporate operations. As with occasional transfers, in a group move environment the employees were provided with a home finding trip; and for the first time secured the services of housing advisors or coordinators, from an organization like Homerica; the provision of new area information material; rental losses; home sale assistance; loss on the sale of their old residence; provision of home loans; the movement of household goods; and the reimbursement of the costs of the final trip.

The final group covered what was provided to newly hired employees. As had been the case since the beginning of the industry the primary reason for providing new hires with relocation expenses is to create an even playing field in the search for required talent. This group of employees received very basic relocation assistance including household goods cost reimbursement. A typical allowance was equivalent to one month's salary. The corporations also paid for a home finding trip to the new location.

The final study of the fifties decade was done by John Kinley for the Conference Board of Canada in 1959. In his paper entitled *Company-Paid Moving Expenses for Individual Employees*, the level of relocation assistance for employees of corporations in Canada was reviewed. The report reviewed the relocation practices of 110 companies with offices throughout Canada. Of all the research papers released during the decade, this was the first to indicate that if the employee moved for his benefit, the company was less likely to pay for the relocation. This idea continues to the present based on some of the more recent Internal Revenue Service opinions.

Mr. Kinley discovered in the process of his research that the Canadian firms tended to offer their employees relocation assistance which covers home finding trips if they occurred within certain distances from the old location, rental losses, home sale assistance, final trip assistance, and the movement of household goods to the new location.

Economic and Cultural Environment

From an economic and cultural perspective, the fifties decade was a mixed bag. After recovering from a war economy, for several years we suddenly found ourselves involved in another armed conflict half a world away in Korea where we still have troops stationed today. Within two years of the start of the decade, the citizenry chose to elect a war hero as President of the United States, Dwight David Eisenhower, who promised to run this country on an era of bi-partisan cooperation. At the time the country also saw the efforts of a young legislator in Washington schedule a series of hearings under the guise of the Committee on Un-American Activities claiming that in every aspect of our society there were cells of Communists who controlled the outcomes of the input of society. A number of high profile entertainment individuals were black balled due to their refusal to testify in this effort. The direct result was that those who created the material we heard, saw, and read no longer represented the traditional elite. As the decade continued, the movement we called *pop art* began to appear in places such as Greenwich Village and Haight-Asbury. This climate that corporations dealt with everyday had its effect on relocation because with the changing nature of the American worker, some of their demands for relocation assistance also changed.

The decade's relocation activities would not be complete without looking at the experiences of Don McPherson who was discussed in Chapter One. As stated earlier, McPherson moved from the Midwest to the New York metropolitan area. Upon arriving in the area, he found that there were no available services to allow a transferring family to get acquainted with the new area. It took visits to seventy-five communities before he found an area that he and his family felt comfortable with. After this disastrous move he saw the need to provide a service which would help corporate employees get settled into their new communities. In 1955, McPherson started Homerica. This company was the first true home counseling business licensed to provide services in all fifty states. The plan was to be able to provide counseling to the families prior to the move and then turn them over to real estate agents in return for a referral fee. The Homerica program was the start of the realization of the need for a smooth national process for assisting transferees with the moves to a new location or destination location.

3

1960

~

1969

There is a common saying that "if you remember the sixties, you weren't there," but we need to remember because this was probably the most dynamic decade for change in the relocation industry. The 1960's introduced the era of the baby boomers (born between 1946 and 1964) to the workforce. It was the period when the third-party relocation management firms came into existence and changed the whole process of dealing with transferees and their problems. It was the decade when the world was faced with the assassination of a President and an ongoing war in Southeast Asia.

Creation of an Industry

The decade's impact on relocation began with an individual by the name of Ferdinand Vincent Marzullo III who was an undergraduate economics student at the Wharton School at the University of Pennsylvania. He graduated in 1960 after completing his thesis entitled "The Problems and Expense of Transferring Employees." Providing some of the research and data for his thesis was empirical research done by John Huggins. Huggins surveyed many of the New York Area corporations as to their interest in providing relocation services for their employees. The results of this report led John Huggins to found the American Relocation Service with Mr. Marzullo. The American Relocation Service, started in 1961, was designed to help families who were facing relocation to new areas handle the various issues they faced through the assistance of a network of qualified real estate brokers. It became the second real estate broker network operating in this country after Homerica in the previous decade. At its height, American Relocation Service was working with between one hundred and one hundred twenty real estate brokers representing two-thirds of the metropolitan areas in the country.

Based on the data from the Marzullo thesis, John Huggins truly felt that his program was unique to the relocation process until he met Don McPherson. Three years after starting American Relocation Service, John Huggins made the decision to close the business and join the staff of Homerica as the second male employee. This occurred prior to the signing of the contract between Homerica and Western Electric (see discussion below).

One of the most significant events of this decade occurred in 1964. At this time, a member of the tax department at Western Electric/ American Telephone and Telegraph made the suggestion to top management that there might be a win-win situation available if the company could hire an outside vendor to handle the sale of homes for employees who were being relocated. First for the employer, they would free up staff time that was devoted to personal matters within the transferees' lives. At the time, the prevailing attitude was that the corporation had no place meddling in the personal lives of their employees unless there was no other solution. This meant that there was more time that could be devoted to the human resource issues within Western Electric/American Telephone and Telegraph. For the employee, it meant that for the first time since the industry began they could have a way to dispose of their old residence without unnecessarily worrying about the details. Based on the suggestion from the tax department, Western Electric/American Telephone and Telegraph approached Homequity and Don McPherson and inquired whether, if the employee could not sell his or her home within ninety days McPherson would then purchase the home. McPherson's response created two milestones in the development of the industry.

The first milestone was the determination of how the corporate client would be billed for relocation services. McPherson's only hesitation was, How would the purchase be funded? In response, American Telephone and Telegraph took McPherson to see a contact at their financial institution, Banker's Trust in New York, for the purpose of establishing a line of credit that could be used to purchase these homes. Bankers Trust said they would establish the line of credit, but only if Western Electric and American Telephone and Telegraph would cover both the indirect and direct costs of the program. The program that developed had Western Electric/American Telephone and Telegraph agreeing to pay twenty-one-and-a-half percent of the value of the home as the cost of the program. The program costs involved not only those costs directly attributed to a certain property – such as property taxes, maintenance, and utilities – but also a portion of the costs involved with running the relocation management company. At the end of each month, the relocation company totaled the expenses they had paid out for office rental, telephones, postage, electricity, salaries, and other costs of maintaining the company's operations. The total operating expenses were then divided by the number of homes in inventory resulting in a per house value of the operating costs. The value was then multiplied by the number of homes each client had in inventory. The resulting amount represented the amount that the corporate client was invoiced for that particular month. This was the introduction of indirect expense billings within the relocation industry. As a result, Western Electric/American Telephone and Telegraph contacted Don McPherson at Homequity and Dan Hanrahan, who was a real estate broker from New Jersey, who combined to begin the first home purchase program in the country.

The second milestone involved the question as to how the relocation management companies would value the employee's home when the relocation management company purchased the residence. The question became complicated in that the goal of the program was to assist the employee in making the move without increasing the stress of the relocation. The result was that the partners in the program turned to an appraisal association for their definition of the market value on a piece of property. This definition stated that **Fair Market Value** *is defined as that price at which a purchaser would be willing to pay for a piece of property considering that all parties were knowledgeable and free from any coercion.* This basic definition of the fair market value for a piece of property is still in effect in the relocation process today.

Research Activities Increase

The corporate interest in exploring the benefits of relocation continued through the completion of a number of research projects into the changes of relocation policies from the earlier decade. Dr. Weston Edwards completed one of the first studies beyond the Marzullo thesis while he was employed at Donaldson, Lufkin, and Jennerette. The study was completed for the management of the financial investment firm to explore the impact of relocation services on the recruiting needs of corporate America. Based on the results of this study, Weston Edwards was encouraged to leave the world of investment banking and enter the fledgling relocation industry.

Karol White completed another study in 1964 for The American Management Association that was entitled *Reimbursing Personnel for Transferee Relocation.* This was followed in 1966 by an additional study into the *Real Estate and Other Assistance for Relocating Employees.* The latter study was actually a compilation of a number of articles which appeared during the period of 1960 through 1966 in the Conference Board publications.

In Chapter Two reference was made to a 1956 Conference Board study entitled "Company Payment of Employee's Moving Expenses" in which the Conference Board surveyed two hundred seventy-two corporations as to their level of assistance when they asked an employee to move for the benefit of the corporation (see page 37). While only four years had passed, the members of the National Conference Board were interested in determining whether the policies discussed in the 1956 report were still valid. The results of the survey found that thirty-seven additional corporations decided to offer relocation services to their employees compared to the earlier study. Like the 1956 study, this study reviewed the same three areas – individual moves, group moves, and new hires. This was done in order to maintain an equal playing field between both studies. In the review of the individual transfer category, the study found that the wording of the new policies applied to any employee who was asked to move by the corporation. However, this became the first introduction of relocation benefit levels being delivered based on the employee's level within the company. If we fast-forward the clock to the current decade we find that this policy is still in place in many corporations today.

The policies generally stated that the moving expenses were reimbursable only if the employee was asked to move for the benefit of the corporation. An Internal Revenue Ruling would further clarify this concept twenty years later. While the requirement was not a matter of law as yet, some of the new responding corporations placed a distance limit on the reimbursements. This distance requirement depended either on a mileage criterion or a nebulous criterion, which stated that the travel time to the new job had to be excessive. Carrying the limitations a little further, a small percentage of the respondents in the new study limited the time period in which the employee could seek reimbursement for the relocation costs. As today, there were incidences where the employee had to leave the family in the old location for some period of time after the employee moved. Equally true is the fact that in some of these occurrences the employee came to the decision that the move was not in the best interests of the family in the long run.

About eleven percent of the respondents had actually included wording in their relocation policies which stated that, if the employee resigned or was released from employment, the corporation would not reimburse for the costs of returning to the family. Among the other policies' components, many of the corporations tried to help the employee in the decision process by counseling the employee on the tax and financial implications of the move. The idea was that this would be completed prior to the employee and the family saying they would take the position and the re-

The provision of relocation benefits actually have formed a full cycle consisting of lump sum allowances to direct reimbursement of expenses, to guarantee against loss, to loss on sale, to in home purchase program to third party program to lump sum allowance.

sulting move to a new area. It was also a period where some corporations introduced the idea of paying a lump sum allowance to the employee to cover the costs of the relocation.

The next area looked at by the study was the use of time for the employee to go to the new area to seek a place to live. In the earlier study, most of the corporations allowed the employee and spouse to go to the area to find housing. Four years later, only eight corporations had added pre-move trips to their policies. Basic policy in the 1960's allowed for one home finding trip on the part of the spouse.

One critical issue involved with the relocation of employees is how to handle moving an employee who is tied to a residence due to a rental agreement, which lays out the conditions under which a lease can be cancelled. The study found that the number of policies, which reimbursed for any losses incurred when an employee broke a lease, had increased from the 1956 study. The prevalence of this policy component had risen from just under half of the corporations to two-thirds of the corporation responding to the survey.

One of the most difficult issues in any move is the disposition of the old residence. As with the other policy components, this area had also shown dramatic increases in the prevalence of its use between the two studies. Two-thirds of the respondents to the 1960 survey indicated that they have changed their policies in this area to include assistance in selling the home. Remember that this change occurred before the advent of the home purchase programs within Western Electric. The policies offered a range of options from the corporation acting as the selling agent to an offer to purchase the home at the appraised value of the property. In conjunction with the home purchases, corporations also looked at the issues surrounding the sale of the home at a loss due to the forced sale caused by the relocation. A loss on sale occurred when the employee, out of necessity, accepted a contract on the property that was less than what he paid for the home originally or was sold for less than the appraised value of the property. The corporations involved in the study chose to handle the reimbursement either through a lump sum allowance designed to cover not only the loss on sale but also the various incidental-moving expenses that might arise out of the move, or they paid a percentage of the depreciated investment in the property. Many of these methods continue today if a loss on sale is involved.

While we are still early in the home purchase spectrum, corporations, to a small degree, were looking into the feasibility of assisting the transferee with the purchase in the new community. One of the hardest parts of moving to a new area is duplicating the current lifestyle in the new location. Part of this process is finding, funding, and closing on a new home that meets the needs of the family. Recognizing this, corporations began the process of making home loans to the employee by guaranteeing the loans secured from a local financial institution. In structuring these loans, the corporation could choose to charge the employee market level interest, a reduced interest percentage, or no interest at all. On short-term loans the corporations typically charged no interest. The amount of the loan was based on the equity in the old residence. In essence, they told the bank that if there were a problem with the loan, they would ensure that the financial institution would be paid what was due. Some corporations were not willing to go that route, so they began reimbursing employees for some of the costs involved in getting the loan.

The last category of individual transfer costs that the study reviewed was that of the expenses of getting to the new location. First off, almost every corporation in both the 1956 and the 1960 study covered the cost of getting the family to the new location. These expenses include the actual trip, the relocation of automobiles, and the cost of moving household goods. As is true today, many of the corporations began to pay for the full cost of packing, transporting, and unpacking of the household effects. While they pay for moving the belongings, most of the corporations also provide insurance to cover any damage of those shipments. The next question posed to the corporations is, What happens if I arrive there and my home is not available? The corporation's response was to state that in most cases they would cover the expense of storing the belongings in a moving company's warehouse until such time as the transferee can get access to their permanent new residence. One aspect of the relocation policies is that if you provide one benefit component, it opens the door for another area of expense. This area is no different. If we pay for storage-in-transit, then the family is going to need a place to stay while their new residence is prepared. The reimbursement of temporary living for the employee usually came with no qualifications or time restrictions as long as they could show that it was a necessary expense to get the employee to the new area. The difference comes about when the family is involved. The family's relocation allowance for temporary living is restricted to around one month in duration at the most.

The transfer scenario with the greatest impact on the family is when the husband is transferred, and the family for some reason must remain in the old location. We know from many studies over the years that commuter marriages do not typically work. The corporations in the study were allowing the employee to return home on visits to see the family.

The second area that this study reviewed was the "group moves" scenario. This occurs when the corporation moves a segment of the operation to another area with the current employee levels continuing. As this was early in the process, most corporations had no group move policy in place. While we had entered the era of the high-mobility population, corporations were not yet on board with the concept.

The last category included in the study involved the hiring of brand new employees from outside the corporation. Among the corporations that had changed their policies to cover new hire expense over the previous four years, the 1960 study found that a much smaller number had decided to cover these expenses. Part of the reason for the drop in number could be that many corporations in the early part of this decade decided not to cover the expenses unless it was necessary to obtain the services of the talent they were seeking.

While the findings of the 1960 study answered some of the questions as to current policy practices, the question still remained as to how far were corporations willing to go to assist employees who had a home to sell. In 1962, the Conference Board returned to the corporate arena to look at this very question. Based on the responses of forty-six large companies, the board looked at the home buyout programs active at the time. For the first time since the mobile society came into existence, demand for housing had eased, making it harder to sell the home without taking a loss. This shift created a dual-edged sword for corporate management. On one side was the corporation who provided no assistance and now found itself forced into doing so because of the demands of employees for assistance in selling their homes. Within the next ten years this circumstance would become a crucial issue for the relocation industry. On the other side of the sword are those corporations who provided financial assistance in a "womb-to-tomb" environment and suddenly found that the home purchase program was getting expensive.

Based on this dual-edged sword, the practices of these forty-six corporations provided a picture of the then-current state of the home purchase process. The Conference Board found that the corporations could

To put this circumstance in perspective, according to the latest data from the Employee Relocation Council, the latest cost figure for moving an employee over and above the salary of the employee was in the range of $60,000. At the time of this study the cost was $3,200.

be placed into three groups. The first group chose to guarantee the transferee that they would cover the cost of any loss on sale. The second group reimbursed certain expenses involved in the sale of the old residence, and the final group felt that it was an intrusion into the lives of their employees — so they chose to do nothing. Of these alternatives the vast majority of firms made the decision to guarantee the home sale price of the employee's home. The real question became what constituted a loss on sale. About half of the responding corporations determined that the loss occurred if the transferee received less than the current market value of the home. The basis for reimbursement consisted of ordering up to four independent appraisals and then averaging the values, which derived the current market value of the home in question. If the transferee sells the home for less than the appraised value, the corporation reimbursed the employee the difference. One tactic to assist the corporations in saving some expense was to change the basis of the market value from appraised value to total investment minus depreciation for the values of the years it was occupied.

The corporations had determined the value for the property and had now come to the point where they had to decide how the homes were sold. These options included the corporation buying the home outright, but only after the employee had tried to sell the home on his own or through a real estate broker for a specified period of time. This was the beginning of the idea of a marketing or acceptance period, which is common to the industry today. During this time period it is possible the corporation would be willing to pay all the selling costs such as the real estate commission and the seller's closing costs that were involved with a contract. The second option was that after the employee had reached the point where they must relocate, the corporations would serve as the selling agent — but they would not take title to the property.

Still another option is that the corporations approached a local financial institution to secure a sale of the property. The bank arranged to sell the property at an average of two or more appraisals. In return for this service, the transferee agreed to provide full access to the bank for a period of four months in order to secure a sale. If the bank is able to obtain an offer which is ninety percent of the appraised value or better, the transferee is obligated to accept the offer of sale. When the home closed if the transferee's net is less than the appraised value the corporation reimbursed the transferee the difference. The primary facilitators of this system were International Business Machines (IBM) and what is now Exxon-Mobil Oil who maintained a network of over fifty banks across the United States for this purpose.

The final option available to the transferee is that the employees can maintain the sole responsibility to sell the home themselves. If this option were chosen, the corporation would reimburse the employee for the selling expenses of the property.

We have talked throughout this section about the corporation reimbursing the employee for the selling expenses of the home. But what is considered selling expenses? The study found that among the items that corporations considered selling expenses were the broker's commission – up to six percent, one month's salary as a lump sum allowance towards the cost of closing fees, appraisal fees, title guarantee expenses, title transfer fees, and mortgage prepayment penalties. Some corporations would cover the carrying costs on the home for up to three months. The exception to these rules seemed to occur in the situation of a group move when corporations were more willing to reimburse the employee for the expenses involved in the move. The final review of the results in this study found that more corporations were involved in helping the transferee sell their home but were encouraging the employee to take the responsibility for getting the home sold.

One year later, in 1963, the Conference Board began its look into the potential of offering home-purchase loans to employees who were asked to relocate by their employers. What was occurring in many cases was that the transferee found themselves in a position of not having enough funds to make the down payment in the destination area. The solution to this lack of funds has continued through the history of the industry. The offering of home loans to transferees has typically been established from several primary perspectives. The first of these is the offering of loans up to the equity that the transferee has in the old residence using company funds. These loans are usually with no interest and for a set period of time, usually until the old residence sells. At that time, the loan becomes due and payable.

In the case of a really needed talent, the second option open to the company was to loan the employee funds that exceeded the equity the transferee had in the home. In this case, the corporation was likely to charge interest on that portion of the loan that exceeded the equity in the property. Still another alternative was to make available short- and long-term loans to enable the transferee to purchase the new residence. The conditions differed depending on the circumstance and the corporation. Typically in a short-term loan scenario, the corporation would lend up to ninety percent of the home's equity, interest free for the first few months, and then charge interest at a rate approximately five percent a year payable on a monthly basis.

The final option for the corporation was to go out and get a financial institution to agree to lend the transferee the required funds for a down payment. The loan was made directly to the employee with the corporation guaranteeing that the loan would be repaid. Despite the corporation's commitment to repay the loan if the transferee defaulted, the transferee was still responsible for the interest on that loan. The 1963 study found that the use of loans for transferring employees to secure new housing was becoming more prevalent. This practice continued well into the early 1980's when interest rates were at an all-time high.

Within one year of the signing of the Western Electric/American Telephone and Telegraph contract with Homequity/Potere, the Conference Board returned to the issue of assistance to employees who were transferred and owned their own home. In March of 1965, the Conference board issued the report of their newest findings in this area.

One of the changes that occurred after the introduction of home purchase programs was that the corporations, to lower the financial risk of their relocation programs, began to encourage the employee to sell the home themselves with the help of a real estate professional. The goal of the corporation in providing this assistance was to minimize the inconvenience and disruption of the transferee's life. While this was still the goal, asking the transferee to assume this responsibility defeated this same goal. The solution was that the corporation went out and secured the services of one of the independent real estate concerns that had begun to come into existence at this time. A more in-depth review of this phenomenon will be found in Part 2 of this book dealing with the development of the relocation departments within the real estate brokerage community.

Another method of avoiding involvement with hard-to-sell properties was to change the method of how the loss on sale was figured. As you will remember, a few pages back we mentioned that the primary way to calculate the amount of the guarantee was to get a current appraisal. That appraisal became the fair market value. If the transferee sold the residence for less than the appraisal, the corporation sent the transferee a check for the difference. In order to lessen the burden on the corporation, some corporations changed the formula for calculating the loss on sale to one based on the *invested value* of the property. Taking the original price that the transferee paid for the residence and adding the total closing costs involved and the value of the capital improvements that had been placed in the home during their ownership calculated the invested value. From the calculated value the corporation deducted the depreciation from each year of residence based on a figure of three percent per year. The thought behind the change was to convince the employee that they should sell their homes themselves.

Relocation Tax Implications

As in the 1950's decade, the Internal Revenue Service continued to make its views on relocation known through the various Revenue Rulings and Private Letter Rulings that it issued. In the first of five Revenue Rulings issued during this decade, Revenue Ruling 63-77 (1963-1 C.B. 177) dealt with the allowances provided to a prospective employer for expenses incurred for an employment interview. In this case, a manufacturing company in one state invited an individual residing in another state to visit the main office to be interviewed for possible employment. The corporate taxpayer agreed, in advance of the trip, to pay all expenses that were incurred during the trip. Under the agreement, the corporate taxpayer paid the cost of round-trip transportation and the cost of the individual's meals and lodging during the trip. The Internal Revenue Service determined that based on the facts above, the payments in question were not remuneration for services rendered or to be rendered in an employment situation. Based on that assumption, the Internal Revenue Service stated that these reimbursements were income under the definition of wages in the Tax Code. This opened the way for a company to use these reimbursements to entice a candidate to come visit the headquarters operation and review the options to relocate to the new location. Relocation benefits were beginning to truly be a cost of doing business.

The next pertinent Revenue Ruling was Revenue Ruling 65-158 (1965-1 C.B. 34) in which a corporate taxpayer inquired as how to treat allowances or reimbursements paid by an employer to or on behalf of an employee transferred from one official station to another for permanent duty for the expenses of the employee which are related to the move. In the case under review, the corporate taxpayer paid the employee for the costs of the preliminary trips to locate a suitable residence, the amount by which the net selling price of the former residence fell below the appraised value (loss on sale), closing fees on the sale of that home, closing costs on the purchase of a new home, charges for connecting and disconnecting appliances and utilities, alteration and installation of rugs and draperies in the new home, and fees to obtain drivers' and auto licenses. The Internal Revenue Service found that these items were by their very nature essentially personal rather than a business expense of the employer. Therefore, these reimbursements were considered income to the employee.

A year later the Internal Revenue Service issued Revenue Ruling 66-41 (1966-1 C.B. 233), which looked at the question of employment agency fees. In the early days of the recruiting field, it was common for the candidates to pay the agency fee when they were seeking new employment. In this case, the corporate taxpayer agreed to reimburse the employee for these costs only after the completion of a specified period of service. The corporate taxpayer contended that this reimbursement was for an expense incurred by the employee while undertaking the employer's business. The Internal Revenue Service determined that these reimbursements were in fact wages under the tax code. However, the employee was able to deduct the cost of the fee from his or her wages provided the tax law allowed the transferee to itemize his or her deductions.

The last Revenue Ruling of the decade was issued in 1967 as Revenue Ruling 67-48 (1967-1 C.B. 50). The question before the Internal Revenue Service was whether the amount paid by a taxpayer as liquidated damages to a former employer for breach of an employment contract qualifies as a business loss. The employment contract provided that in the event of failure on the part of the taxpayer to render the entire period of obligated service, the employee would be liable for liquidated damages in a stated amount. In the case under review, the taxpayer rendered about a quarter of the required time. The Internal Revenue Service found that since the amount of liquidated damages paid by the taxpayer to his or her employer is attributable to compensation received for services rendered, such amount qualifies as a business loss. The deduction is allowable in the year paid but only if the taxpayer itemizes his deductions. The partial importance of this Revenue Ruling is that in some aspects it lays the groundwork for the use of payback agreements that came into vogue several decades later in the history of this industry.

Economic and Cultural Environment

Earlier in this chapter, the comment was made that this decade was probably the most dynamic decade within the industry for change. It was a decade with a wide range of emotions within the country. Many who will be reading this work will have no perception of the era because they were not there to experience it. This was a decade of both great promise and of great apprehension. This was the decade of Camelot. It was a decade that promised a new future and a new expectation for all the members of society. The mantra of the era was *Ask not what your country could do for you, but what can you do for your country.* It was a decade in which, on a late fall day in Texas, Camelot came to an end with the ruthless assassination of a young president of the United States. If this was not enough, by the end of the decade two more prominent figures in the effort to secure equal rights for the entire citizenry would also meet the power of the assassin's bullet. Within five years of the assassination of John F. Kennedy, we would lose both his brother Robert F. Kennedy and Martin Luther King, Jr. The electorate after this would elect as the next leader of this country a president who would later be forced out of office due to a scandal based on a break-in at a Washington D.C. apartment complex.

It was a decade in which for the first time legislation was passed which promised equal opportunities for every citizen. This was brought about by the passage of the Civil Rights Act, the creation of the Gay Rights Movement, and the National Organization of Women. To assist the average citizen to achieve the American dream, Congress created the Housing and Urban Development Department, which was commissioned to develop programs to assist the lower income members of society to be able to buy a home of their own. Along with all the other events of this decade, following the promises of Camelot, this country sent the first man into space with the sub-orbital flight of Alan Shepard, Jr.

On the other hand, the despair began to set in because it became clear that we were bogged down in another war, as if this country was only happy if we were at war somewhere at all times. Viet Nam became a real place on the other side of the world. We had been there before with Korea, but this was a different type of conflict. Many of the Baby Boomers began to be involved in protests against the war, which would come to a head in the next decade.

By 1964, with the assistance of the National Association of Realtors,

Taken from the Inaugural address of John F. Kennedy as President of the United States.

the interest in the changing economic environment in which we lived caused a group of corporate representatives to get together and create a trade association for this new industry we called *Relocation*. Called *ER-REAC*, or the *Employee Relocation Real Estate Advisory Council*, it began with the urging of representatives from Kodak, Federal Mogul Corporation, General Electric, General Mills, Hercules Power, Kraft Foods, Massachusetts Mutual Insurance, Walker Manufacturing, Goodrich Rubber, Consolidated National Gas, and Packaging Corporation of America. ER-REAC became a forum in which the corporations could come together to discuss the issues that were facing the corporations in relocating their employees. Many of these issues were the same issues reported in the various research studies discussed earlier in this chapter.

This was the decade when another milestone was reached, as California became the most populated state in the union. California also heralded a change in our cultural lives as what we knew as Pop Art changed to Op Art. Op Art was propelled by the introduction of drug use by some members of the younger generation. This is part of the reason for the adage which opened this chapter. Many of that generation found solace in the use of mind changing drugs that reportedly gave them a new outlook on the world around them. They also began to experiment with new lifestyles such as communes in California and the far West. It was also the decade in which the Boomers escaped from the problems of the world by gathering on a small farm in upstate New York, creating a phenomenon which has lived in the lore of this country ever since – we are talking about Woodstock, of course.

Circumstances in the world created a mood for protests against the inequities of society. Women who felt that they were being treated as second-class citizens founded the National Association for Women. Blacks who felt that they weren't making any progress with civil rights began protests and riots to make the point that they needed to be included in society as much as the white folk. In response, the US Supreme Court heard the arguments and responded to a case by stating that mixed race couples deserved the same treatment under the laws of the land.

In the economic arena, the Federal National Mortgage Association, which was providing federally backed mortgages to lower income citizens, portioned itself into two separate agencies, thus creating the Government National Mortgage Association. At the end of the decade, Congress amended the US Tax Code by adding section 217 to the text. This revision laid out some of the requirements for the taxation of relocation benefits which are in place today. These requirements included that the move had to be for the benefit of the employer, the move had to be for a certain time period, and it had to involve a certain distance from the old location. If you return to our discussions of the policy research from the 1950's into the relocation industry, the requirements are very similar to the basis of many of the corporate policies that were reviewed earlier. In an advance look at some of the technology we use today as almost second nature, this was the decade of ARPA or the beginning of the Internet. Today, we use this vehicle for almost everything we do in communicating with our transferees.

4

1970

~

1979

As we begin our look at the third decade of the relocation industry, the climate in which the corporations were operating in was a period of much turmoil and tribulation. The nature of the transferee was changing. The economic market was going through some rough times, which would come to a head at the transition to a new decade.

The New Transferee

The transferee of the 1970's represented the first time when the Baby Boomers finally made it to some of the boardrooms. It was an era when the understanding was that if you wanted a future with your employer, you moved if you were told to move. Unfortunately, this led to some highly mobile employees moving on the average once every two years. In 1972, Vance Packard took note of this trend in his book *A Nation of Strangers*.

The basis of Packard's book was that the high mobility rate among American workers has resulted in a decline in the family and the loss of ties to the community in which we live. The foundation for these beliefs stems from five trends that he saw as the direct result of the above mentioned results.

The first of his causes was the uprooting of the individuals. As stated above, this was the time in the business world that you moved when you were told to move or your career suffered as a result. As the fast track employee moved up the career ladder, it was not abnormal for an employee to move once every twenty-four months or less. It has been said in a number of studies that it takes the average transferee about three years to fully settle into a new community. So just as employees got to the point of settling in, the corporation decided to move them again.

The second of Packard's causes was the result of community upheaval. The 70's decade was the era of the families moving out of the city and into the suburbs. The odds were that the people you worked with were not necessarily your neighbors in whatever leisure time you might have had. This led your employees to begin to stay pretty much to themselves. There was no feeling of community amongst your neighbors.

The third cause was the change in the housing options within the community. Toward the end of the last decade, but more prevalent in this one, the trend was away from the building of single family residences and more toward the building of condominiums and other forms of multi-family housing. The problem is that such living arrangements let you get to know your immediate neighbors but not those in the surrounding buildings. If you are like many individuals, you may not get friendly even with your adjoining apartment dwellers. There tends not to be any sense of community among the residents. When you consider that the transferee and the family are under enough stress anyway from the move itself, this disassociation tends to aggravate the situation.

The 1970's was also a time when the number of hours worked by the average employee began to rise. When the local employer goes to operations around the clock and that employer dominates the area, what happens is the employee gets up in the morning, goes to work, comes home, has dinner, and then goes to bed. The next morning they start the process all over again. What results is that there is little time left for anyone to fit into a new environment. The family becomes isolated in their own little quality world.

The final cause of this trend that Packard outlined was that families became fragmented. If you will remember in Chapter 2, we discussed that prior to World War II the tendency was that the family stayed within several miles of each other for their entire lives. The result was that the holiday times were a time of great celebration. As the family got together to enjoy the time, those present represented each and every viable generation of the family from the youngest child to eldest grandparent. It was a time when the children listened in earnest as the elders related the stories of past holidays and events within the family. As the 1970's arrived and we began to move employees every two years to some other far out location on the planet to provide them with the necessary tools to climb the corporate ladder, this mesh of generations began to decline. Now when the holidays arrived, the youngest child talked with the elder of the family by telephone rather than being in their presence most of the day.

All of these factors led to the evolution of a new type of transferee. Unlike the transferees before them, they now were demanding increased relocation benefits. The transferee expected that more would be done to assist in the transition to the new area. The corporation was expected to help with the financing of the relocation and to cover the expenses incurred during the move. The transferees expected to come out of the relocation in the same condition financially as when they went into the move.

Tax Implications by the Internal Revenue Service
The Internal Revenue Service kept up its record by releasing no less

than eighteen Revenue Rulings covering the time period from 1970 to the end of the decade. They covered a wide spectrum of issues, with one in particular becoming the basis for the future of the relocation industry.

The first ruling was issued in 1970 as Revenue Ruling 70-188 (1970-1n C.B. 133). It looked at the question of whether the relocation payments to an employee who was separated from his employment would be treated as unemployment benefits. In the case before the Internal Revenue Service, the corporate taxpayer had established a supplemental unemployment benefit trust for the active employees. Section 501(c) (17) of the Internal Revenue Code of 1954 exempted the trust from Federal Income Tax. The purpose of the trust was in case the personnel needs lessened causing the involuntary release of a number of employees. Some of these employees were offered positions in other operations of the company and relocated to the new area using the funds in the trust. The Internal Revenue Service held that because the benefits were paid as a consequence of impending involuntary separation and because they were used to prevent the separation, they did constitute supplemental unemployment compensation and, therefore, were considered as supplemental unemployment compensation benefits. The impact of the ruling is that these benefits were now considered taxable income to the transferee. The question for the corporate taxpayer becomes how do they handle the trust payments in the future. Obviously, if they are trying to keep the transferee whole by not putting them out of work, it changes the impact on the transferee.

The next ruling occurred also in 1970. It was Revenue Ruling 70-250 (1970-2 C.B.66). The question posed to the tax authorities was whether a serviceman could deduct the expenses incurred in moving his dependents to his new duty station in a foreign country even though the dependents have 90-day tourist visas and the move was in violation of the duty station's housing rules. This ruling is one of several that looked at the relocation of Armed Forces personnel in the period before they were given the right to relocation services. The taxpayer in this case asked the Internal Revenue Service to advise as to whether the member of the Armed Forces is entitled to the moving expense deduction for his dependents under Section 217 of the Tax Code. The service member was an enlisted man with less than four years of active military service who was transferred to a new duty station located overseas. He applied for and received the moving expense reimbursement for his dependents. The dependents claimed the former duty station as their principal place of residence and had changed that to the new location. At the time enlisted members of the Armed Forces with less than four years experience of active duty were not eligible to move their dependents at government expense when changing an assigned duty station. Further, to complicate the situation, there was a housing shortage at the new location, so new housing control procedures were introduced which allowed families to live off base only if they moved at government expense. In addition, the family was permitted to rent or reside in housing that was not approved by the duty station. While the Armed Forces had not as yet gotten clearance for relocation services and would not for some time, the Internal Revenue Service review became one of the first cases to look at the implications of Section 217 of the Tax Code. What the Internal Revenue Service stated was that Section 217(a) provides that there shall be allowed a deduction of moving expenses paid or incurred during the taxable year in connection with the commencement of work in a new principal place of work. It further stated that in section 217 (b) moving expenses are defined as the reasonable expenses of moving the household goods and personal effects from the former residence to the new location. It also includes the traveling expenses to get there.

The section further states that the expenses of a person other than the taxpayer are likewise reasonable if they have the same principal residence address at both locations and are a member of the taxpayer's household. Section 217 (c) of the same code provides that one of the conditions for the allowance is that during the twelve months immediately following the relocation, the employee must be a full-time employee for at least thirty-nine weeks. Their finding was that, based on the definitions in the law, the service member is entitled to the deductions for the move. Essentially, the Internal Revenue Service has stated that if the move meets the requirements of the Code, then the expenses are deductible.

The basis of section 217, which became law in the previous decade, is that the move must meet three tests. The first is whether the move is for the benefit of the employer. The move must be due to a change in the location of the work required. The second test is one based on time as stated above. The employee is required to work for thirty-nine weeks during the following twelve months. The final test is a distance requirement in which the distance moved must meet certain criteria. If all the tests are met, then the taxpayer is entitled to the relocation expense deduction.

One of the frequent questions which has been discussed within industry circles has been that of how do we handle the personal effects of the transferee during a move. The Code is quite clear that personal effects are included in reasonable expenses. But the caveat that the Internal Revenue Service looked at in the next ruling, which was Revenue Ruling 70-625 (1970-2 C.B. 67), is how to handle un-reimbursed expenses. In this case an employee on his way from New England to Colorado to start a new position stopped off in Massachusetts and picked up some additional new furniture for the home. The individual taxpayer was not reimbursed for the expense of moving the furniture. The Internal Revenue Ruling stated that because the furniture was purchased en route, it was not deductible under the tax code.

In another indication of the views of the Internal Revenue Service, they published Revenue Ruling 70-656 (1970-2 C.B. 67). In this case, an employee qualified for the deductions for moving expenses under Section 217 of the Tax Code. The individual taxpayer argued that the vehicle he used to move his household goods and personal effects should be subject to depreciation for the wear and tear on the vehicle in driving to the new location. The Internal Revenue Service stated that the question of depreciation was not one covered by Section 217 but rather Section 167. However, the new referenced section states that in order to claim the deduction for depreciation, the property must be used in the taxpayer's trade or business or held for the production of income. Since in this case none of these conditions were met, the Internal Revenue Service rejected the deduction for the depreciation of the automobile. The ruling provides a view from the Internal Revenue Service's perspective that while there is allowable consideration for the reimbursement and deduction of relocation expenses, it does have its limitations.

Following the above-mentioned rulings, we experienced an ebb during which the Internal Revenue Service issued no applicable rulings. This ebb continued to 1972 when they issued the next ruling. In 1972, the Internal Revenue Service reviewed a question pertaining to the consideration of moving expenses that were paid to an employee. In this case advice had been requested about whether the moving expenses paid by an individual that were attributable to the employee's business could be used in determining the net operating loss deduction. In the case before the Internal Revenue Service, an individual who had accepted a position in the last quarter of the year had used a cash receipts and disbursements method of accounting. He filed his federal return as required by law. Within a year he was moved to another location in the same capacity and for the same employer. Because of the move coming within so short time, he found that his ordinary and necessary business expenses exceeded his income. This ruling is important because it was one of the first to look at someone operating out of a non-corporate facility to look for relief from the tax burden created by the move. The question arose several times in the years since regarding how to handle the relocation expenses of individuals who work essentially from their own homes. The Internal Revenue Service held that the employee was entitled to taking the full deduction for the moving expenses in determining his net operating losses.

The Internal Revenue Service in 1972 also issued what has become one of the most important revenue rulings that they released during the entire history of the industry. Before we review the impact of this revenue ruling, let's review the normal process involved in a home purchase program within corporate America. Regardless of whether we are talking about an in-house program or one that has been outsourced to a third- party relocation management company, the process is essentially the same. The corporation usually hires two independent fee appraisers who appraise the home to arrive at its fair market value. The employee is then given the opportunity to try and beat the corporate offer by marketing the home themselves. At the time of listing the property, the homeowner (transferee) includes in the listing agreement an exclusion clause to the listing. This exclusion clause states that the transferee retains the right to sell the home to his employer or the relocation management company with the cancellation of the listing and no commission due. The corporate offer is then signed and the transferee signs over beneficial title to the relocation company. In the process there is no commission paid to the corporation by the transferee or the corporation.

In 1972, Eli Lilly asked the Internal Revenue Service for an opinion as to whether the employee had to account for the realized gain on the sale to the corporate employer. Based on this issue, the Internal Revenue Service issued Revenue Ruling 72-339 (1972-2 C.B. 31). In the case presented to the Internal Revenue Service, Eli Lilly agreed to purchase the home of any employee being moved to a new work location. The basis of the agreement was that they would purchase the home at a value equal to the value determined by appraisers familiar with the market. Eli Lilly selected three qualified and independent real estate appraisers who would make separate appraisals of the property. These three appraisals were averaged, and the employee was offered this appraised value as the fair market value for his home. Following the agreement, the average created a gain on sale situation for the employee. Despite the employer purchasing the home, none of the closing costs imposed on the seller were borne by the company and no sales commissions were paid or incurred by either party. As became common in third-party transactions, the employer and employee neither paid nor incurred any commissions within the transaction where the employee sold the home to the employer. The Internal Revenue Service informed Eli Lilly that the employee would still be accountable for the gain on the sale of the home, but that no part of the transaction would give rise to income as compensation for the amount of the real estate sales commission that the employee neither paid nor incurred as part of this transaction. The impact of the ruling laid down the ground rules for the development of the industry to the present day. Consider that for the first time, the Internal Revenue Service, in the issuance of this public revenue ruling, confirmed that the process we had been following since 1964 was correct. Corporations could now offer to their employees the purchase of their home if they could not sell it in order to facilitate the pending relocation.

In 1975, the Internal Revenue Service took its first look at the issue of the rapidly organizing global business environment. In Revenue Ruling 75-84 (1975-1 C.B. 236), a corporate taxpayer asked for advice on whether, under several scenarios, the moving expenses and the reimbursements for those expenses were includible as gross income. In each scenario the taxable year for the employee was 1972 and used the cash receipts and disbursements method of accounting. In the first situation, the employee, who was a citizen of the United States and the employee of a domestic employer, was notified in late 1971 that he was being transferred to a foreign operation of this employer. He relocated and spent the entire calendar year of 1972 living as a bona fide resident of the foreign country. In return for accepting the position, he was reimbursed for $6,000 in allowable moving expenses. During this year his only compensation was that paid by his employer in the amount of $19,000. In the second situation, a citizen of the United States was employed by a domestic corporation living in a foreign country and qualified as bona fide resident of such foreign country for his entire taxable year. In the following year, the employee was transferred to the United States to work for the employer's domestic operations. His employer reimbursed the employee's moving expenses to the United States. In the third situation, a United States citizen who was employed by a domestic employer in a foreign country qualified as a bona fide resident of that country. The following year the employee returned to the United States and went to work for another corporation other than his employer while overseas. The first employer, however, did reimburse his relocation expenses. The final scenario took a slight twist. In this case a United States citizen employed by a domestic employer in a foreign country qualified as a bona fide resident of the foreign country. In the year following, the employee made the decision to return to the United States and retire. His employer reimbursed him for his moving expenses. Nine separate sections of the Internal Revenue Code came into play as the Internal Revenue Service issued its opinion. The final opinion represented a diverse look at each of the scenarios. In the first scenario, the opinion presented said that the reimbursed moving expenses are chargeable against income from sources outside the United States. In the second scenario the moving expenses were considered chargeable against income from sources within the United States due to service in a foreign country. Likewise in scenario three, the income derived from service in a foreign country is considered gross income.

In the final scenario, we need to re-look at the conditions present in the situation. The employee had worked for a corporation overseas and was returning to this country to retire. Section 217 of the tax code specifically says that in order to claim a deduction for the moving expense reimbursement, the employee must be moving for the benefit of his employer and moving to a new location of work. Since he was retiring, he was not moving to a new place of employment and thus the relocation expenses are not deductible.

This ruling led to another taxpayer requesting further clarification of the issues shortly thereafter.

In Revenue Ruling 75-85 (1975-1 C.B. 239), a corporate taxpayer requested advice as to the proper treatment for Federal income tax purposes of the moving expenses for an employee who moved to a foreign country and became a bona fide resident of that country. In the circumstances described in the request, a citizen of the United States who files his Federal income tax return on a calendar year basis left the United States at the beginning of November 1970 and arrived in a foreign country on the same day for the purpose of seeking employment as an employee at a new place of employment in that country. During that calendar year, the employee incurred and paid un-reimbursed moving expenses. He remained as an employee in the new location for the entire following year. During the 1970 time period, he earned no income from the United States. The ruling stated that the employee did in fact have the ability to exclude the reimbursement from his income.

One area of concern at this time was the implications of the distance test of Section 217 of the Tax Code. This issue was the subject of Revenue Ruling 78-174 (1978-1 C.B. 77). Section 217 states that in order to claim the exemption for relocation expenses, the employee must undertake a move which meets the distance requirement. The requirement states that in order to do so, the distance from the old residence to the new place of employment is thirty-five miles further than the distance from the old residence to the old place of employment. For example, if the distance from the old residence to the old place of employment was five miles, the new place of employment must be forty miles from the old residence. In the case before the Internal Revenue Service, a corporation on a full time basis employed an employee for twelve years. As part of a general reduction in force, the employee's employment was terminated. The employee remained for a period of two months and was then employed full-time by another corporation. As a result of obtaining the new job, the employee sold the old residence and made a permanent move to a new home. The distance between the former residence and the new principal place of work is fifty-five miles, thus exceeding by thirty miles the distance from the former residence to the former job location. Section 217 further states that if a new hire had no former principal place of work, then the distance to the new job location must be at least thirty-five miles from the former residence. In its opinion, the Internal Revenue Service found that the distance from the former residence to the new place of work was well within the requirements of Section 217. However, the former residence is only thirty miles farther than the old residence from the former work location. Further, the employee was not unemployed for long enough to be considered entering the workforce. Accordingly, the employee may not deduct expenses from the relocation. The implications are that the relocation professional must be cognizant of the requirements for deducting the relocation expenses in a move.

In still another look at the problems that arise in relocation, the Internal Revenue Service took a look at the decision to leave the family behind in the old location while the children completed schooling. In the case before the Internal Revenue Service, the employer transferred a taxpayer from Los Angeles to Chicago. The decision was made that the spouse and the children would remain in the family home in Los Angeles until the youngest child graduated from junior high school in June of 1977. The employee rented a furnished one-bedroom apartment in Chicago from December 1974 to June 1977. At that time the home in Los Angeles was sold, and the family purchased a new residence in Chicago. On their income tax return for 1974, the employee claimed a moving deduction for traveling expenses in moving to Chicago. The question that was posed to the Internal Revenue Service was whether moving expenses incurred thirty months after the commencement of work were, in fact, deductible. Because the one-bedroom apartment was not suitable as housing for the employee and the family, the home purchased in 1977 was the one considered as the new residence for Section 217 purposes. Therefore, those expenses were deemed to be deductible under the Internal Revenue Code of 1954. This scenario is played out again and again due to the difficulties of moving a family to a new location.

A New Industry Evolves

With the rapid changes within the relocation field, ERREAC began a new chapter. In 1972, they changed their name to the *Employee Relocation Council* to become the first true trade association connected to the industry. The decade also saw the entry of seven new relocation management companies who saw a new outlet for their services. As we will see in the next section, this was the era of the growth of the referral networks within the real estate community. As the industry grew, the Employee Relocation Council also saw the need to refine some of the processes in use. The first area was to try and to find a standardized form for the appraisal. It seemed that every part of the country had its own form that was in use as did every relocation management company. The Employee Relocation Council also started in the 1970's to develop many of the research studies that have become a vital part of the industry knowledge on which many of your department policies are based. This initial research included a survey of relocation policies (1974), New Hire Survey (1975), International Relocation (1976), and Relocation Trends (1977).

This was the era when the funding model of the industry began to change. If you will remember in Chapter 3, we discussed the creation of the indirect expense charge back to the corporate clients at the insistence of Banker Trust. As we approached the mid 1970's, many of the relocation management programs created home counseling centers to assist the transferee with the move to the new location. The way these centers were funded was in part through a new source of revenue for these firms. The theory behind this new source of funds was that the relocation management firm had a guaranteed sale in hand. Therefore, if they delivered this sale to a real estate broker, they should be entitled to some compensation. The result was the creation for the first time of referral fees collected from the real estate community. In the typical scenario, the relocation firm referred a transferee to a real estate broker in the destination location. When the sale was consummated, the real estate broker agreed to pay the relocation firm a portion of the referred side commission. For example, if the purchase price of the new home was $100,000 and the sales commission was set at six percent, then the real estate broker owed the relocation company twenty-five percent of the selling side, or $750.00. As time went on, this would dramatically change the nature of industry.

Economic and Cultural Environment

The economic and cultural environment of this decade was almost as uncertain as was the previous decade. The decade began with the secondary mortgage market creating the third leg of the mortgage security business when the Congress established the Federal Home Loan Mortgage Corporation. This now meant that the secondary mortgage market was comprised of the Federal Home Loan Mortgage Corporation, the Government National Mortgage Association, and the Federal National Mortgage Association. Each of the legs of the market, while having separate responsibilities, had the same ultimate goal. This goal was the issuance of mortgage-backed securities which in turn helped fund mortgage loans for the lower income home purchaser. If we visit their current websites, the sites define who they are and the role they play in the housing market. This is critical to the relocation industry as their mortgage programs help some of the first time transferees locate and purchase that residence when they are moved to a new location. This was also a decade in which the per capita income of the workforce began to increase from a level of $3,177 in 1970 to $7,168 by the end of the decade. This meant that the buying power of the consumer continued to increase. In contrast, this buying power would be compromised as interest rates climbed to record levels.

This was also an era of increased concern about the world around us and the effects of our past practices on the future of the planet. The culmination of this effort was reached when Senator Gaylord Nelson and Denis Hayes began a campaign which ended in the celebration of Earth Day on April 22, 1970. Cities across the country planned both small and elaborate celebrations of the planet we lived on including looks at pollution and other signs of environmental degradation. Along with the Earth Day celebrations, the ongoing protests against Viet Nam and the draft brought renewed confrontation between the protestors and the government officials. This confrontation climaxed with a number of students shot and killed by National Guardsman on the campus of Kent State in Ohio.

The 1970's decade was also the decade in which the typical transferee was an individual who gave everything he had to his career. This probably meant taking home work or working long hours to complete projects that needed to be completed by a certain date. In 1971, Wayne Oates coined a term for this phenomenon and called these workers *workaholics*. His belief was that the employee who fit the image was addicted to the idea of work.

With the economic environment of the decade growing, we saw an increase in the population to a level of two hundred and eight million by the beginning of the decade. The decade also saw the continued migration of the population across the country with the Census Bureau reporting a total of approximately thirteen million interstate moves just during the 1970-71 and 1975-76 portions of the decade. Part of this number was an increase in the relocation level of corporate employees to enhance their career ladder. This was the beginning of the era when the *move every two years* became more commonplace among the young executives. This was the era when the Baby Boomers began to reach the age of maturity and reach into the boardrooms of the country. Most of this generation were either in the workforce already or just graduating from college with their undergraduate degrees and entering the business world with new knowledge of how business works. The decade also demonstrated to us that things could be done in the name of a final result without consideration for the effects on the road to getting there. This was demonstrated through the unfolding of two events during the decade. The first was the goal of showing the world the belief in the cause of the Arab plight by the killing of the majority of the Israeli wrestling team at the Munich Olympics. The other event was the break-in at an apartment complex in Washington to spy on the Democratic Party operations. The complex was called *Watergate*, and it would eventually bring down an American President from office.

On the financial side of the era, the markets were hit hard. By the mid-1970's, the country had entered a recession which would last for two years and witness a decline in investments of forty-six percent and the largest stock market drop in overall value in nineteen years. The country saw inflation rise and an energy crisis hit the country. This was the era of gas lines, where residents would line up around the block to get gasoline at reasonable prices and where you were able to get gasoline only on certain days of the week. It was the time when the Justice Department questioned the size of some of the American corporations, so they filed suit in Federal Court which ended in American Telephone and Telegraph being torn apart into what has been called the *Baby Bells*. By the mid-1970's, the government had also introduced and had passed the Real Estate Settlement Protection Act, or RESPA. It was designed to protect the rights and funds of the consumer buying real estate. The principles of the Act are still in effect today. By 1975, the median price of a home had reached $39,300. This was up from $13,400 in 1955 as discussed earlier on page 33. Three years later the average home in California reached an $85,000 price tag. This trend of California being more expensive than the rest of the country continues to present day.

5

1980

~

1989

This first decade past the half-way point in the development of the industry was a time of great diversity. The traditionalists, as discussed earlier, were beginning to reach the point where they were retiring from the top of American business. It also was a period when the Baby Boomers began to take their places in the corner offices. In fact, many of the individuals that we consider the elders of the relocation industry today began their careers in the industry during this time period. The vacancies created by the retiring traditionalists were being filled by a new generation, which, in the not too distant future, would have a major impact on the workforce. We called this group *Generation X*. The decade also was a very difficult one for the transferees due to the economic conditions that existed in the marketplace as discussed below.

The Economic Environment

This decade represented the end of the Carter presidency and the beginning of the Reagan era, which would last for much of the decade. During our recent national day of mourning for his death, we heard a lot of rhetoric about the great things he did during those eight years in the White House. The Reagan years placed the country once again in its traditional role as the leader of the free world. The Reagan years boosted the country's morale after the tragic Viet Nam war and the disgrace of the resignation of a President due to the Watergate break-in. Americans could once again feel proud of their country and not ashamed that we, in essence, walked away from a battle, and we tried to elect a president based on subterfuge instead of the will of the people.

But at the same time, we have to be cognizant of the downside of the era as well. The Reagan presidency was defined by economic policies which were based on a theory called *trickle-down economics*. The centerpiece of this theory was that if you cut the tax burden of the wealthy, they, in turn, would have more disposable funds to hire more employees so that the lower and middle class members of the citizenry would see larger paychecks. Unfortunately, this theory did not hold true. Despite the outcome, these same concepts are played out in today's economic policies of the 2000 Bush presidency.

In addition, the administration's spending plan was heavily tilted towards the military. Programs that were set up to provide a safety net for the middle and lower class members of the population were drastically cut. Due to spending more than was coming in to the US Treasury, the national debt climbed to a record $2 trillion. This rise in the national debt led to some major drops in the Dow Jones Industrial Averages.

The secondary mortgage market was comprised of the Government National Mortgage Association (GNMA), Federal Home Loan Corporation (Freddie Mac), and the Federal National Mortgage Association (Fannie Mae). These three quasi-governmental agencies sold mortgage-backed securities.

In response to this economic climate, corporations began to assist transferees and other homeowners cope with these rising costs. The financial markets introduced some new programs. The secondary mortgage market introduced the use of adjustable rate mortgages. These mortgages changed rates based on the market conditions at the end of each quarter or some other predetermined time period. Due to the premise that the transferees were considered to be a better risk than the "normal" population, some of the national lenders introduced a set of preferred rates for relocating transferees' new mortgages. In part, these new programs were introduced to combat double-digit inflation that caused interest rates to climb to twenty percent during 1981. The following year the Federal Department of Housing and Urban Development allowed for the free negotiation of the interest rate on the Federal Housing Administration's guaranteed loan programs.

This era also introduced a new term in the business environment. Until this point in the history of American business, our relatives worked for the same employer for 100,000 hours – or their entire working career. With the arrival of this decade, we suddenly heard the term *downsizing* (or *rightsizing* depending on which book you had just read). Whatever term you put on it, this was the beginning of the loss of many jobs in the workplace.

The belief was that you could make an enterprise become more attractive to the stakeholders by cutting expenses through lowering payroll costs. Rightsizing was accomplished by looking at the corporate structure and eliminating what was believed to be excess positions. The rule of the day was to run the corporation as lean as possible. While there is no evidence that this downsizing ever really cut expenses, it continues today as a primary strategy for reducing costs when economic times are tough. One of the negatives of the downsizing trend was that while the number of jobs decreased, the workload did not. This resulted in the workloads of the remaining employees increasing.

Another aspect of the economic environment of the 1980's was the government decision that telephone service in this country was a monopoly. The US Department of Justice began dissolving the monopoly, which resulted in the 1984 break-up of the Bell system nationwide. What was then an operation that consisted of a parent company and a collection of subsidiary firms was faced with the prospect of initiating the process of creating what we now term the *Baby Bells*. American Telephone and Telegraph was forced to give up all of its operations except Bell Labs, Western Electric, and the long distance operations. This is of importance because Western Electric, as we stated in Chapter 2, began using an outsourced home purchase program.

Much of what we have discussed to this point has been confined to the domestic relocation arena. As the decade reached its mid-point and worked its way toward a close, the world saw a new perspective. US Corporations, with the drop in costs of every aspect of doing business, found that they were no longer involved in a strictly domestic business. Instead, it became increasingly clear that the market the clientele came from represented a global perspective. In a dramatic change, the world, and not just your immediate neighbor, was the market. The 1980's employee had to understand how the business practices of a business in Japan or China influenced the way they did business in this new market. A really good picture of this evolution in business can be found in Thomas Friedman's *Lexus and the Olive Tree*, published by Anchor Books in May of 2000. The direct result was that we now had the beginning of the movement of transferees to the far corners of the globe to fulfill the requests of this new market for our products and services. It also was the start of the era of learning how we would handle the expatriate once we brought them back to this country following the conclusion of an assignment.

The Relocation Industry

The 1980's decade was one of excitement and great changes if you listen to the "elders" of the industry today. It was the era when many of them began their careers in a rapidly changing business model designed to assist with the needs of the corporate transferee in an era of turmoil as interest rates reached all time levels.

To get a clearer picture of the times, we need to return to the research that was being done into the policies for the relocating employee. In 1981, the Conference Board for the first time since their 1966 research asked its membership about what benefits they were providing to their employees considering the nature of the economy at the time. In their report, entitled *Personnel Practices II: Hours of Work, Pay Practices and Relocation*, authored by Harriet Gorlin, the Conference Board discovered that almost seventy percent of the membership sometimes transferred lower level ex-

Baby Bells consist of Nynex, which covers New York and New England; Bell South, which covers Virginia south to Florida; Ameritech, which covers the Midwest; Southwestern Bell; US West; and Pacific Telesis, which covers California and Nevada.

Lexus and the Olive Tree was written by Thomas L. Friedman who was a reporter with the New York Times and was originally published in the hardcover edition by Farrar, Straus and Giroux (ISBN 0374185522) and later in paperback by Anchor Books in May of 2000 (ISBN 0385499345).

empt employees. Interestingly enough, despite the tough times, about seventy percent of the members reported no relocation refusals.

When Gorlin turned from the frequency of the moves to the actual policy components, she found that corporations were providing, as a basic rule, two expense-paid house hunting trips, full payment of the costs of getting the employee and the family to the new location, full payment of the household goods movement, thirty days of interim housing for the employee, and reimbursement of selling costs or lease breaking penalties.

Less than twenty-five percent of the members were providing any assistance for the difference between costs from one area to the next, and about half of the corporations assisted the employee with the added tax liabilities generated by the move.

The report also indicated that forty percent of the respondents introduced for the first time assistance with finding new employment for the spouse in the new city. The final finding in the report was that more than half of the membership had one policy for current employees and a different policy for the new hire.

Many of these new policy components were introduced in reaction to the corporate policies of the competition for the human capital talent. This was done so that the corporation could remain competitive in the job talent aspect of their businesses. These new policies created further unique and innovative programs being offered to the transferees.

By mid-1982, interest rates climbed to an all time high of twenty-one percent on a thirty-year fixed rate mortgage. The impact on relocation was significant due to the dramatic rise in the costs of moving. Many corporations began to look for solutions to assist the transferee.

While not calling it by its current name, James Neilson, who worked in the human resources department at Eastman Kodak, created a mortgage interest differential allowance program in 1982. *Mortgage interest differential allowances* are temporary subsidized payments that make up the difference – between the lower rate in the departure location and the higher rates in the destination location – for a limited period of time. The amount of the payment is calculated by subtracting the old mortgage principal and interest from the new mortgage principle and interest payment. The difference is then multiplied by twelve for the months in a year and then times the duration of the allowance. The payments can be made as a lump sum, as a constant payment, or as a graduated payment over the duration of the allowance.

For example, an employee currently has a $100,000 loan with an old loan rate of seven percent (principal and interest = $661), and upon moving to the new location he obtains a loan with an equal mortgage balance with a new rate of ten percent (principal and interest = $870). The lump sum payment would be $7,524 plus gross up. The constant payment would be $209 for thirty-six months. The graduated payment would be $209 per month for year one; $157 per month for year two; and $105 per month for year three. The program would pay an equated premium for the higher payment for whatever period the program called for. As Eastman Kodak's program began to show some success, other corporations made the decision to also offer an identical program.

Starting in the early 1940's, the Interstate Commerce Commission dictated the way the entire household goods industry operated. The Interstate Commerce Commission established a set of tariffs which each household goods company was required to charge, no matter how big they were or how big the client was. In essence, the tariff program placed every van line in the country on the same playing field, since there was no provision for altering the tariffs. Some of the larger van lines began looking for ways to enhance their competitive place in the industry. They got their wish in the form of new legislation passed by Congress. In 1980, the Congress passed two pieces of legislation which changed the way moving companies calculated their fees for their services.

Both the Motor Carrier Act and the Household Goods Transportation Act changed the moving business dramatically. While the Interstate Commerce Commission still established a tariff, the individual moving companies were now able to adjust the tariff based on the services they offered in the marketplace. Moving companies now were able to quote a fee to current and prospective clients based on the services delivered rather than a firm price established by a firm tariff charge. The direct result was that the van lines, which were surviving due to the arbitrary fee set by the government, now had to be able to demonstrate that they could perform better or at the same level as the other companies in the marketplace. The van lines were able, under the legislation, to charge what ever they could negotiate based on the levels of service and performance offered. Discount levels have climbed to the point where, in some cases, the move barely brings any profit to the van line after all is said and done.

If you remember back to the start of our journey, reference was made to several Internal Revenue decisions pertaining to the movement of members of the Armed Forces. Despite these rulings, it was not until the passage of PL 98-151 during this decade that the Congress finally saw fit to allow the government agencies to begin to offer formal relocation programs to government agency employees. The very first government agency to utilize this new authority was the Federal Bureau of Investigation. This contract concept was designed by Harvey Auger, Kevin Russell, and Bob Nagel from PHH Homequity utilizing a fixed fee contract, which meant that the services were delivered based on a negotiated fee basis. The fees were reviewed, usually on a quarterly basis, and the fixed fee was adjusted based on the experience of the program. The basis of the government contract is still in use today with the government contracts.

The decade was also the beginning of a push for more complete disclosure of property conditions than the industry was used to dealing with. The first factor to undergo strict disclosure was the use of UFFI or Urea Formaldehyde Foam Insulation. In 1982, the Consumer Product Safety Commission issued a warning that UFFI was considered to be a dire health risk. The use of this material involved the injection of a mixture of the foam and the formaldehyde into the cavities of the wall where the mixture expanded into a foam to insulate the home. The problem was that in some cases the formaldehyde eventually emitted a gas which could be hazardous, causing both an allergic reaction and respiratory problems. Within a year of issuing this warning, a US Court of Appeals threw out the warning and removed a ban on the use of the product in homes. By this time it had fallen out of grace anyway, and so it no longer became an issue.

Another disclosure issue that appeared at this time was the presence of asbestos in the older homes of many of the transferees being asked to relocate. Asbestos was used as both an insulation material and in the construction of some of the more common household amenities such as ceiling and floor tiles. The concern became critical when the asbestos over time became very brittle to the point that when touched, it crumbled in your hands. To remove the asbestos was tremendously expensive.

Of equal concern was the discovery of radon gas in residential buildings throughout the country. Radon gas is the direct result of uranium in the soil going through its natural life history. The problem came when the gas was created within a structure with little or no ventilation. The resulting gas would prove to be the direct cause of respiratory problems in certain members of the population. The problem was such magnitude, the US Environmental Protection Agency recommended that every home in the country be tested for radon levels within the structure.

The final major disclosure issue of the decade concerned a threat that came about due to our own practices. Many corporations in the country began the process of eliminating waste material from their manufacturing processes by dumping them in landfills across the country. As the material leached into the soil, the land around these dumps became contaminated with a multitude of toxic waste, which affected the health of the surrounding population. A number of these waste dumps also had a direct effect on the ability of a transferee to sell their home. In fact, the author attended a seminar in the mid-eighties where we discussed a home in the Northeast that sat next door to a toxic waste dump that was not disclosed by the appraiser, and the relocation management company could not determine why the home would not sell until they discovered the presence of one of these dumps seven hundred feet from the home.

Another change to the industry was that as the decade progressed, corporations began to look towards control of relocation costs. One method of doing this was refusing to pay indirect expenses of the relocation management firm. In order to recover the lost revenue, the relocation management firms turned to other sources for this income. Their initial target – and still one of their sources of income today – is charging real estate brokers a referral fee for the business that the relocation companies refer to them. Another source was creative pricing for the services that were delivered. This could be a certain fee based on volume or the type of property involved. The relocation companies began the practice of looking at homes that were out of the norm for the neighborhoods and pricing them differently than the typical subdivision home.

As did many other industries, the relocation industry underwent many changes during this decade. The industry experienced the creation of many new companies offering relocation services. For example, Relocation Realty Service Corporation which was started in 1970 by Ed Carroll and Carroll Hassler was sold to Control Data and their Commercial Credit Corporation subsidiary. In addition many real estate companies began to create relocation subsidiaries as they broadened their service packages.

The companies that entered the industry at this time were designed around several different models. Many of the firms were centralized and serving a niche market. These companies would service their clients from a single location. The belief was that the client was provided with a higher level of service to the transferees. As will be seen in Chapter 7, many of the larger relocation management firms moved toward this model in the aftermath of 9/11.

The second model was one in which the relocation management firms operated from the premise that it was better to take the services to the client instead of having the clients come to them. The result was that many of the larger and mid-sized firms began to set up regional offices around the country. Typically, they were found in New York, Dallas, Los Angeles, Chicago, and the location of the corporate headquarters of the firm.

Tax Implications

As with the previous decades that we have reviewed, the Internal Revenue Service continued to make their impact on the industry during the 1980's. Their rulings covered a wide range of issues, which directly looked at how corporate America treated the relocation of their employees.

One of the first rulings by the Internal Revenue Service was Private Letter Ruling 8016098. In this ruling, The Internal Revenue Service was asked by a corporate taxpayer to discuss the tax consequences of relocation payments to the corporation, the shareholders, and the transferees.

The corporate taxpayer in this scenario is a diversified manufacturer with over eleven thousand employees nationwide who had contracted with a relocation company based in California. Under the terms of the agreement between the corporation and the relocation company, the relocation firm agreed to the purchase and resale of the homes of the corporation's employees within three hundred sixty days. In return for this service, the corporate taxpayer agreed to compensate the relocation firm in accordance with a fee schedule, which was based on the type of transaction, the value of the home, and the direct selling costs. The employee who accepts the program will sell his home to the relocation firm based on the average of at least two appraisals. Upon acceptance of the offer, the employee will execute and deliver to the relocation firm a contract for sale and other forms and documents, including a deed-in-blank concerning the residence. The relocation firm will advance to the employee an amount up to the total equity in the property for use in purchasing a new residence. The corporation did not propose to pay any of the sales commissions or any other obligation normally deemed to be the seller's responsibility. The Internal Revenue Service, in their decision, based their findings on their Revenue Ruling 72-339 and said that, under the terms described above, the employee does not recognize any taxable compensation for the fees paid to the relocation firm, and, therefore, the corporation is not liable for any employment taxes.

This ruling was followed by Private Letter Ruling 8134089 which was issued on May 28, 1981. This Letter Ruling looked at the question of the contracts with third-party relocation firms and how those costs are treated from a tax standpoint. In this case, the corporate taxpayer has a program to help their transferred and newly hired employees with the sale of their present homes and the purchase of a new residence. As part of the program, the corporate taxpayer entered into an agreement with a relocation firm to assist with the purchase of the old residences. The process involved – according to the information that was provided to the Internal Revenue Service – the corporate taxpayer advising the relocation firm that an employee was being relocated. The relocation firm immediately ordered two independent appraisals of the employee's home. The employee had the option to select the two appraisers based on a list of authorized appraisals provided by the relocation firm. If the two appraisals varied by more than five percent of the higher value, a third appraisal would be ordered. In the case of an out-of-variance appraisal, the three appraisals would be averaged to arrive at the value of the property.

Upon receipt of the appraised offer, the employee was provided thirty to forty-five days in which to accept the offer by executing the contract of sale and returning it to the relocation firm. The relocation firm then had twenty-four hours to execute the contract of sale. If the employee decided to try and sell the home himself and gets a bona-fide offer within the forty-five-day period at a price higher than the appraised value, the employee was required to notify the relocation firm immediately. The relocation firm would then immediately amend its value to equal the offer from the outside purchaser. The employee would then be given two days to accept the amended offer and a total of ten days to submit the contract of sale to the relocation firm.

The fee that the corporate taxpayer pays to the relocation firm is based on a variable performance fee of three percent of the appraised value of the property and direct selling costs of 11.3 percent. If the sale is based on an amended value transaction, the corporate taxpayer pays the relocation firm a fixed fee of 1.5 percent of the amended value of the property plus all direct closing costs.

In reviewing this case, the Internal Revenue Service determined that since this process met the conditions established by Revenue Ruling 72-339, the costs of implementing this program do not constitute the payment of moving expenses for the transferee. The Internal Revenue Service further indicated that the principles of 72-339 were equally applicable to Section 82 of the US Tax Code. The relocation firms were, however, told that in those cases where they paid any of the direct home selling costs treated under local law as a custom imposed on the transferee, these payments would constitute income to the employee. Therefore, these payments when they occur are subject to all employment taxes.

In one of the most important decisions of the decade, the Internal Revenue Service issued Published Revenue Ruling 82-204 (1982-2 C.B. 192, 1982-48 I.R.B. 7) on November 29, 1982. Before beginning a review of this decision, it is necessary to lay some groundwork. When a corporation enters into an agreement to purchase a residence of the transferee, it is in the corporation's best interest to have the costs classified as a cost of doing business. In doing so, the costs become deductible as business expenses.

In 82-204, a corporate taxpayer with facilities throughout the country regularly transferred employees to these offices in the course of business operations. In order to assist the employees with the sale of their personal residences, the corporate taxpayer established an employee relocation program. Under the plan, the corporate taxpayer obtained two independent appraisals which were averaged to calculate an offer for the property. During 1980, the taxpayer purchased several homes which were immediately offered for sale to the general marketplace with no improvements made to the property. As has been the policy since the beginning of the process, the corporation had no plans to hold the properties for investment purposes but planned to sell them as soon as the market would allow. The market time on these properties ran from almost overnight to in excess of a year before a suitable buyer was located. The corporate taxpayer felt that this scenario meant that any expenses incurred were ordinary business expenses and should not be treated otherwise. During 1980, the corporate taxpayer realized both gains and losses from the sale of the homes. The Internal Revenue Service determined that, according to Sections of the Tax Code, the homes sold to the taxpayer were capital assets within Section 1221. This determination was based on the fact that the transferee's properties were not purchased and sold as an integral part of the corporate taxpayer's business operations. As a result, the capital losses had to be offset by capital gains. There is a window of opportunity under this scenario of five years in which the capital gains have to be applied against capital losses, or the value of the deduction disappears.

Two years later, in April of 1984, the Internal Revenue Service issued Private Letter Ruling 8428031. While this can't be used by any taxpayer except for the one asking for the ruling, it does give us insight into how the Internal Revenue Service was thinking about these issues. In this particular case, the corporate taxpayer asked the Internal Revenue Service to rule on the employment and income consequences of a relocation program in three separate scenarios.

In this case, the relocation management firm upon authorization from the corporate taxpayer ordered three independent appraisals. Each appraiser was required to provide two estimates of the fair market value of the home. The first estimate of value was based on the receipt of a cash offer, and the second one was based on FHA or VA financing. The fair market value was calculated by averaging the two highest appraisals. In the case where the appraisals were outside of a five percent spread, a fourth appraisal was ordered, and the three highest appraisals are averaged for the value. Upon the calculation of the value, the transferee is provided with a forty-five- day window in which to decide if they are going to accept the offer to purchase the home. If within the forty-five-day window the employee accepted the offer, the relocation management firm and the employee created an assigned sale transaction. The relocation management firm paid all the costs and charges in connection with purchasing, holding, and reselling the property. The corporate taxpayer paid all the direct costs of the program to the relocation management firm. The corporate taxpayer also paid the relocation management firm a service fee based on a percentage of the resale price of the home. The property was listed with a real estate broker chosen by the relocation firm.

Based on this description of the existing program, the corporate taxpayer asked the Internal Revenue Service to issue three rulings. The first dealt with whether the amounts paid to the relocation management firm were considered income to the extent that they were not treated as costs imposed on the employee under local law. Second ruling asked whether the amounts paid to the relocation firm which are attributed to costs treated as imposed on the seller under local law are compensation and thus wages to the extent that a corresponding deduction is not allowed to the employee under Section 217. Finally the corporate taxpayer asked for a ruling on whether the payments they made to the relocation management firm were deductible as ordinary and necessary business expenses under the Internal Revenue Code.

The Internal Revenue Service held that when the relocation management firm buys an employee's home, no part of the transaction results in income to the employee as compensation for a real estate commission that is neither paid nor incurred. However, as had been stated in Revenue Ruling 72-339, the employee is responsible for the realized gain from the sale to the relocation management firm. Further, the Internal Revenue Service determined that where the relocation firm pays any of the direct home selling costs treated under local law and custom as imposed on the seller, the employee does receive gross income. In those cases where the scenario lends itself to the above-described events, the employee is subject to withholding for the income. Finally, the Internal Revenue Service agreed that the expense charges billed by the relocation management firm to the employer are, in fact, ordinary and necessary business expenses.

In 1984, the Internal Revenue Service also received a request from a corporate taxpayer concerning the consequences of their relocation program. Once again, the Internal Revenue Service issued a subsequent Private Letter Ruling dealing with the issues involved with a program. In this case Private Letter Ruling 8430085 looked at a corporate relocation program in which the corporate taxpayer established a relocation program to assist their employees involved in a move.

In the corporation's inquiry, the question is posed about the tax consequences if the typical process of purchasing the home is changed. In the corporate taxpayer's particular situation, they want to amend the program so that the corporation will purchase the transferee's home at the highest value based on an appraisal, an established appraisal, or the net investment value. To assist in determining the value of the property, the corporation will seek the opinion of three independent fee appraisers and then average the three values. This became the appraised value of the property. To begin the program, the corporation planned to purchase the homes of the eligible transferees either based on this appraised value or use the net investment value, which ever was higher. The net investment value was calculated by adding up the purchase price of the home and adding in the closing costs, capital improvements, major maintenance costs, real estate taxes, and insurance premiums that have been paid by the transferee. From this figure the corporation deducted an allowance for the interest earned on the investment and to reflect a charge for the rental value during the period of ownership. Once the offer is made, the transferee had a sixty-day window in which to accept the offer. If during the sixty days the employee received an offer for the home in excess of the corporate offer, the value would be amended to agree with the higher market value.

Once again, using the arguments presented in Revenue Ruling 72-339, the Internal Revenue Service looked at each of the questions posed by the corporate taxpayer. In the first ruling, the Internal Revenue Service stated that the expenses paid or incurred by the corporation under its employee relocation program are not considered income to the transferee and, therefore, not reportable as wages.

In the second ruling in which the corporation purchases the home using the net investment method of determining the value, the picture changes somewhat. The tax authorities have long held that as long as the purchase price by the corporation represents the fair market value of the property, the purchase price is not considered income. However, in this case, if the net investment property is in excess of the fair market value, each dollar in excess of the appraised price is considered income and, therefore ,taxable to the employee.

In the third part of the request, the Internal Revenue Service found that to the extent that the costs paid by the corporation in the process of purchasing the residence are treated under local law and custom as imposed on the corporation, the amounts are not considered income to the transferee. Further, if the costs are treated under local law and custom as a burden of the seller, they are not considered taxable income if the corporation believes that the employee is entitled to a deduction under the Internal Revenue Act of 1954 Section 217.

In the final question from the corporation, the Internal Revenue Service ruled that real property taxes, which are properly applied to the corporation, would be deductible by the corporation. This also applied to the maintenance and utility costs that were paid by the corporation after the transferee vacated the property. The only area that was not in agreement with this concept dealt with the interest paid on the assumed mortgage, which the Internal Revenue Service said they were not in a position to rule on at the time. In fact, they went on to rule that the mortgage payments on the residence were capital expenditures.

This decade was fairly busy with activity from the Internal Revenue

Service. In 1985, the Internal Revenue Service received a request from a corporate taxpayer inquiring whether an employee recognized compensation as the result of the corporation or relocation firm purchasing the employee's home and, if so, is the corporate taxpayer liable for the withholding of the payable taxes.

In Technical Advise Memorandum 8522002, which was issued in February of that year, the Internal Revenue Service once again looked at this question. The issue was presented to the Internal Revenue Service by one of their field agents who was auditing a corporate taxpayer and was confronted with a situation in which the corporate taxpayer frequently transferred employees between offices in different locations. To make the relocation easier, the corporate taxpayer hired a relocation management firm to provide a full range of professional services in connection with the move.

Net Cash Return Value contained certain conditions. First, the offer had to produce this greater then net cash value. Net Cash Return was determined by taking the offer from the ultimate purchaser and subtracting the commission and closing costs to reach a bottom line figure. Second, the ultimate buyer has received or has been assured that he will receive adequate financing to consummate the sale. Finally, the offer is at a fixed price and not dependent on the occurrence of any, even such as the sale of another home to assist in encouraging homeownership across the country.

In doing so, the relocation management firm followed a procedure which required the corporation to notify them that a transferee was authorized to receive the service package. Following receipt, the relocation management firm, with the permission of the employee, ordered two independent fee appraisals of the property. Upon receipt of the two appraisals, the values were averaged and became the purchase offer by the corporation.

Following the appraised value offer for the property, the employee was sent a contract of sale for the property with a forty-five-day period in which to accept the offer. If, during this forty-five-day period, the employee receives an offer which contains a greater net cash return than the corporate offer and meets certain conditions, then the corporate offer would be amended to the new value.

The first condition of the program was that the outside buyer had received or had been assured that he would receive adequate financing to consummate the sale. In other words, the purchaser needed to demonstrate in writing that a mortgage lender provided the transferee with a notice of pre-approval for financing on the home the transferee is planning on purchasing. In conjunction with the same track, the final condition was that the outside buyer's offer was at a fixed price and was not contingent on any outside circumstance. This meant that the transferee was encouraged not to look at an offer for the home that was contingent on the sale of the buyer's home.

Making the assumption that all the conditions are met, the employee must properly execute all of the terms of the sale. One of the responsibilities was that the transferee needed to terminate any existing listings with a real estate broker. In order to achieve this, the initial listing agreement with the broker contained an exclusion clause,\ which called for the cancellation of the listing if the transferee sold the home to the relocation management firm or the employee's employer.

After the closing, the relocation management firm would try and sell the home to an outside purchaser. In order to achieve this sale, the relocation management firm would use the resources available in the community, including a real estate broker. In the case of an amended value transaction, the discretion of the relocation firm allowed them to use the broker that had the home listed at the time of the sale to the relocation company.

Remember that a Technical Advise Memorandum is nothing more than advice to a field agent. In this case, the Internal Revenue Service's National Office reviewed all the facts that were presented to it and advised their field agent that, based on seven different sections of the Tax Code, it was their opinion that since the employee arranged for the sale of his home at a price in excess of the appraised value for the property, the proceeds of the sale constituted taxable income to the transferee. It appears from the case information that the employee then assigned the sale to the relocation management firm who paid the fees associated with consummating the sale. It was further evident from the case materials that all the parties to the transaction believed that, despite the presence of an exclusionary clause, the real estate broker expected that it would receive a commission upon the presentation of a bona-fide purchaser for the property. The Internal Revenue Service believed that they had no other choice but to rule that the payment of the real estate commission was, in fact, an indirect reimbursement of the employee's moving expense.

Based on the culmination of these issues, the national office advised the field agent that the only available conclusion was that the payment of the realtor's fees constituted indirect reimbursements of the employee's moving expenses and were includible in the employee's income. The employee was also in receipt of wages due to the directed offer situation (i.e. payments in excess of the appraised value), in the equivalent of the amount of the tax liability protection which was provided by the corporate taxpayer. This was based on the fact that at the time of the reimbursement, it was not reasonable to believe that the transferee met the other requirements of Section 217 of the Tax Code.

In a related issue, the Congress of the United States during this time period passed three separate tax reform acts that affected the way the individual taxpayer completed their returns. Of these, the most significant was the Tax Reform Act of 1986 which was considered to be one of the major accomplishments of the Reagan Administration.

The Tax Reform Act of 1986 presented a mixed bag of effects on both the individual relocating transferee and the corporations requesting the move. The purpose of the act was to simplify the tax structure of the country. In order to achieve this goal, the legislation called for a reduction in tax rates. This was coupled with strategies to broaden the tax base. The attempt to broaden the tax base was achieved through incentives to home ownership such as raising the amount of the home mortgage deduction. The downside was that in order to achieve this goal, the incentives available for rental properties such as apartment buildings was phased out. With the phasing out of the rental housing incentives, the legislation also ended the deductibility of the interest on consumer loans, as well as state and local taxes.

The final intention of the Tax Reform Act of 1986 was to end certain tax exemptions and preferences. Among the preferences that were removed were such items as the taxation of unemployment taxes and the change in the way relocation expenses were treated.

Prior to 1986, relocation expenses were a line item on the 1040 tax return in which you deducted these costs before the calculation of adjusted gross income. The Tax Reform Act of 1986 moved this deduction to the backside of the return. This moved the deduction from being of use to *all* taxpayers to one that was of use only if the taxpayer itemized deductions. By moving the deduction for moving expenses to a below the line location, it no longer played a role in the calculation of the adjusted gross income. What this meant to the transferee was that the tax code stated that anything paid to or on behalf of the transferee was considered to be income. However, unless deductions were itemized, these deductions could not be claimed on an annual return.

Another requirement of the Tax Reform Act of 1986 was that all transactions involving the sale of a residence had to be reported to the Internal Revenue Service by the closing person or entity. This reporting requirement involved telling the Internal Revenue Service who sold the home, the address of the property, and the price for which it was sold. The Act also dictated that the closing person withhold a certain amount of the sales price if the new purchaser was not a citizen of the United States.

A final factor in the changing tax environment in the 1980's was that the transferee began to complain about the added impact of the requested transfer on them and their family from the tax perspective. Many of the relocation benefit components actually added to the transferee's tax burden, and they began asking the employer for assistance. These requests led to the creation of a formula in which the employer assisted the transferee with the tax burden by *grossing up* the salary to cover the tax liability of the moving expenses.

6

1990

~

1999

The journey that I began to take you on starting with page 15 has now reached its final full decade. The decade that began on January 1, 1990 was entirely different from the decade that we ended when we went to asleep the evening before. Granted these changes may not have been that abrupt, but it very quickly began as the new decade began. The characteristics of this new decade were spread across our entire spectrum of existence.

The world was different. With the efforts of President Ronald Reagan, the cold war ended. We no longer were concentrated in a battle between the United States and the Soviet Union. The information revolution and the Internet were beginning to move into full swing. Thomas L. Friedman, in his book *Lexus and the Olive Tree*, states that

> there are many ways to sum up what the Information Revolution and the three democratizations did to the marketplace... First it greatly lowered the barriers to entry into almost every business, by radically lowering the costs for new entrants. By lowering the barriers around companies, the information revolution also brought them closer to their customers.

This meant that the market for the products and services of our corporations and of those of other countries rapidly expanded worldwide as the cost of doing so declined.

Business was different. Relocation costs began to escalate to the point where a full package could cost as much or more than the transferee's annual salary. Corporations began to look for ways to lower these costs. One way they achieved this goal was to turn the purchase of relocation services into a commodity. Thomas Friedman in *Lexus and the Olive Tree* defined a *commodity* as

> any service, product or process that can be provided by any number of firms and the only distinguishing feature among these firms is who can do it cheapest. It means your profit margins become razor thin, you will have dozens of competitors and all you can do is make that product or service cheaper and sell more of it than the next guy.

The other side of this coin was that more and more corporations were now opening business operations in many foreign countries around the world.

Because of the presence of the Internet, every corporation with access to the Web was now a global player. Friedman went on to point out that

> Every big multi-national needs to try and sell globally, in order to make up in volume for shrinking profit margins, and it needs to try and to produce globally in order to keep manufacturing costs down and remain competitive. This has led to more multinationals investing in more cost-lowering production facilities abroad.

He further states that

> In the era of globalization, multinationals increasingly need to expand overseas, not because it's the only way to be an effective local producer in these countries, but because its now the only way to become an effective global producer.

The impact on these corporations was that in order to start these local producing facilities, they found a need to begin to transfer employees not only from New York to California but increasingly they were now sending them to Paris, London, and other locations around the globe. This meant that a whole new system for selecting who was going to be asked to undertake the assignment had to be created. This meant that corporations had to establish a whole new management track for those who now gained experience on an international level and needed to fit back into the domestic operation when the assignment was completed.

Financially the world was different. The beginning of this decade saw the United States faced with the highest deficit on record until the administration of George W. Bush entered the picture. It would not be until the middle of a new administration that we would see the deficit turned around to a record surplus through a change in the way government treated the needs of its citizenry. This change in direction on spending led to a period of a shortage of qualified human capital for many corporations in the country. It was the height of the dotcom boom of corporations whose business models were based on effectively utilizing the power of the new world of technology to spread the message of the Internet to the world. These factors would change the way some governments responded to the world during the 1990's and still do today. It was also the time for the introduction of many of the trade agreements being introduced, specifically the European Free Trade Zone and North American Free Trade Act.

This was also the era when the country's savings and loan industry crashed. Represented by some of the country's oldest financial institutions, due to some out of the ordinary loan practices and the hiding of some of the returns on those investments, the savings and loans were hit hard during this period to explain why things were done the way they were. The leaders of many of the larger savings and loans ended up in prison because of the practices of the industry.

During the decade, Congress passed several pieces of legislation that would have a dramatic effect on the transferees that we served every day. First, Congress passed a tax reform act, which returned the deductions for moving expenses to an above the line deductions, thus allowing all transferees to be able to deduct the moving expenses on their tax returns. On the downside this same legislation removed the deductibility of a set amount for house hunting, temporary living, and real estate from the deductible costs of a move.

The same piece of legislation changed the treatment of capital gains. Prior to this a homeowner could take a one-time deduction of $125,000 at age sixty-five for any capital gains they had earned from the sale over their lifetime. Further, they were required to purchase a home of equal or greater value if they moved in order to defer the sale to the sixty-five-year point. Under the new rules, a couple could now deduct $500,000 if they lived in the residence as their primary residence for two out of the past five years.

The Internal Revenue Service began the decade with one of several rulings on relocation benefits for transferees. In a case filed with the Tax Court in March of 1990, Azar Nut Corporation asked for a decision on the treatment of the sale of transferee's homes. The history of this case demonstrates the complicated nature of the industry that we have chosen to participate in.

Mar Nut Company maintained a principal office in El Paso, Texas. They filed timely US Corporation income tax returns for the tax year ending June 29, 1985. In 1980, the Azar Nut Company was a family-owned business and was primarily managed by two brothers. As they approached retirement age, they made the decision to lessen their participation in the management of the company. The company determined that in order for it to maintain and improve the business following their retirement, it needed to employee an experienced top executive to be trained to replace the two brothers. Consequently, pursuant to an employment contract, the corporate taxpayer purchased for the full market value of $285,000 a house owned by a terminated executive employee. The company immediately tried to resell the home but was unable to do so for a time period of twenty-four months. At this time they sold the home for a $111.336 loss. Azar Nut subsequently claimed a loss on their return as an ordinary loss.

The Internal Revenue service claimed that the loss was not valid since the house was a capital asset of the Azar Nut Corporation. The basis for their decision can be found in a couple different areas of the Tax Code.

Section 162(a) of the Tax Code states that there shall be allowed as a deduction all the ordinary and necessary expenses paid or incurred during the taxable year in carrying on any trade or business. The Tax Court disagreed, since the amount that was paid to the terminated employee represented nothing more than the fair market value for the home. Further, the court found that there was no record of any premium being paid above the fair market value for the property. Therefore, the employee did not recognize any compensation for the sale of the home. The court also found that the loss represented the actual decrease in value of the property following the termination.

Section 1221 of the Tax Code provides for the definition of a capital asset. It defines *capital asset* as property held by a taxpayer but does not include property used in the taxpayer's trade or business. The Court found that the property in question did not meet the intent of the code as it pertains to being used in the business. The final summary opinion of the tax court was that the property in question was not and is not being used in the furthering of the business – so it is a capital asset.

Four months later, the Internal Revenue Service handed down an additional ruling affecting the relocation industry. Private Letter Ruling 9041046 was the response to an inquiry from a relocation management firm and the treatment of real estate broker information requirements arising out of the management firm's activities in connection with the management relocation plans of a client employer.

The program was intended to assist certain employees in selling their homes when they are asked by their employer to relocate. In each case the employees eligible for the assistance discussed here are those who are transferred from one management position to another management position in another city. According to the program, the employer would obtain two appraisals of the employee's home. If the two values were within a five percent spread, the average of the two values is considered to be the guaranteed value of the home. If the values are outside of the above indicated spread then a third appraisal was obtained, and the two closest values were averaged to obtain the guaranteed value.

Once the value is obtained then the relocation management firm deals with the employee and the home on behalf of the employer. All the costs and benefits associated with the mechanics of the program are billed or paid directly to the employer. Under a separate compensation arrangement, the relocation management firm is paid by the employer for the delivery of their services.

Once the relocation management firm receives the offer, they send the employee the offer and explain the three options available to the transferee. The first option allows the transferee to accept the offer directly. If this option is selected, the transferee must execute a deed to the property-in-blank and sign a power of attorney to sell or otherwise deal with the home and return the documents to the relocation management firm. The employee is then given a period of ninety days in which to vacate the property. This is accomplished with neither the relocation management firm nor the employer taking title to the property.

For the second option, the employee assigns to the relocation management firm an executed contract of sale for the home. The employee must present such a contract within sixty days from the date of the guaranteed value. Upon being assigned the contract, the transferee receives the equity in the home based on the guaranteed value. The relocation company closes the property under the terms of the contract, and the closing costs are paid by the relocation management firm, except for those costs that are not typically paid for by the seller. Once the property closes, the transferee receives the remaining equity in the property, reduced by the closing costs that the employee is still responsible for. The employee is also responsible for the costs of ownership up until the day the home is vacated.

In the final option, the employee is eligible for reimbursement of certain costs but does so without the involvement of the relocation management firm, in essence rejecting the guaranteed value offer for the home.

The question before the Internal Revenue Service was, Under the new changes in the Tax Code from the Internal Revenue Tax Reform Act of 1986, who is responsible for reporting the information from the transactions regarding the sales?

The Internal Revenue Service ruled that for option one, the relocation company constitutes a purchaser of the employee's home for federal tax purposes and, therefore, is the real estate reporting person under Section 6045. When the home is ultimately sold to the outside buyer, there is no reporting required because the relocation management firm was a corporate seller.

Under option two where the contract price exceeds the guaranteed value, the assignment of the contract and the execution of the backup documents accepting the offer to the relocation management firm does not constitute a transfer of title, and so there is no required real estate reporting. When the assigned contract closes, it does in fact constitute a real estate closing in which the employee is the seller, and so the closing is subject to the real estate closing provisions of the Tax Code. If the contract price under option two does not exceed the guaranteed value when the property is sold to the relocation management firm, it is considered a purchaser for federal tax purposes and must report the real estate transaction. Finally under option two, when the assigned contract is closed, no real estate reporting is required because the relocation management firm is a corporate seller.

Beginning in the late 1980's and continuing throughout this current decade, one very critical issue was the question of what to do with the new hire who came on board, received the training that the employer provided, and then went off to greener pastures. In response, many corporations created payback agreements. We will talk about these instruments more in depth in Part 3 of this work when we look at all the relocation policy development. For our consideration at this juncture, we have to be aware of Private letter Ruling 9050053 which was issued in September of 1990. The question posed to the Internal Revenue Service dealt with the consequences of the employer provided moving expense program for its employees. In order to be competitive in the marketplace, the employer provides various allowances for the moving expenses incurred by the both newly hired and current employees in connection with work-related transfers. The company may either pay the expenses directly or reimburse the employee for the expenses. Under the terms of the agreement with the employee, if the employee chooses to leave the employment of the company within a specified period after the transfer, the employee is required to repay the company for the allowances that were provided for the move.

Based on these criteria, the Internal Revenue Service ruled that any direct or indirect payments or reimbursements to an employee for moving expenses that are not deductible under Section 217 and which are included in the employee's compensation are not wages for withholding purposes. Further, the ruling stated that for those payments to the employee that would be deductible – but for the dollar amounts imposed by Section 217 which are included in the employee's compensation – would be considered wages for withholding purposes. This same condition applies to those expenses that do not meet the definition of moving expenses that are included in the compensation paid to the employee.

The final part of the ruling looked at several other aspects of the indicated program. First, in regards to points on the mortgage that are reimbursed to the employee, the Internal Revenue Service ruled that points that do not qualify as deductible moving expenses under Section 217 are wages even though the reimbursement may be deductible on the employee's return as qualified residence interest. Second, the ruling stated that if the employer pays a third party for the employee's moving expenses that are not deductible by the employee under the Tax Code, the employee may at the time the employee receives the compensation give the employer a check in the amount of the withholding requirements under the Tax Code. The employee also has the right, under written election, to give the employer a check for the additional tax liability provided that all payments to the employer do not exceed the amount of the employee's wages. The only additional caveat stated was that the employee was prohibited from paying the employer for the additional withholding at any time between receiving the compensation and the end of the year. Finally, the Internal Revenue Service looked at the question of the payback agreement. The Internal Revenue Service found that two different scenarios applied to the agreements. Under the first scenario, if an employee terminates employment and repays the moving expenses in the same year as it is received, such allowance is not included in the employee's income as compensation and, therefore, they are not wages. The second scenario concerns the situation in which the employee fulfills the requirements under the payback agreement but provides the repayment in a year other than the one in which the allowances were provided. The Internal Revenue Service stated that such allowances continue to be includible as income for the year that they are received, however such allowances are not wages and the employer should make any adjustments that are necessary.

While the filing date is not provided, about the same time the Internal Revenue Service issued Technical Advice Memorandum 9036003 to one of it's field offices on the subject of whether a corporate taxpayer who contracted with a relocation management company to purchase the homes owned by employees were deemed to have purchased and sold the homes.

In the case being reviewed by the Internal Revenue Service national office, the corporate taxpayer is in the business of selling products and has a number of employees and does business in different locations in the United States. To facilitate the relocation of its employees, the corporate taxpayer has entered into contracts with three relocation management firms for the purpose of purchasing designated employee's homes. Upon being notified of the relocation of an employee, the relocation firm would discuss the potential sale with the employee. Under the program, the employee had a thirty to sixty day window to accept the offer for the property which was based on the completion of an independent fee appraisal. If during this window period the employee was able to secure a bona fide offer from a potential purchaser that was higher than the corporate offer, the relocation management firm would match the offer.

If the transferee accepted the offer, the employee executed a deed-in-blank and received a payment of the equity in the home from the relocation management firm. The relocation management firm then assumed the responsibility of carrying and maintaining the home for sale. In most cases the title for the property was not transferred to the relocation management firm.

While each of the contracts with the relocation management firms differed slightly in their format, each provided that the corporate taxpayer would reimburse the relocation management firm for the costs it incurred and that a service fee would be paid by the corporate taxpayer in addition. Under each of the contracts, if the relocation management firm sold the home at more than the offer, the gain would reduce the amount owed to the relocation firm. Under each contract, the relocation management firm was held harmless from all claims, liabilities, losses, damages, and expenses that were caused by the failure of an employee to fulfill any obligations under a contract for sale.

Based on this scenario, the corporate taxpayer had deducted these expenses as ordinary and necessary business expenses while the district Director of the Internal Revenue Service treated these amounts as nondeductible capital expenditures. After review, the national office provided the opinion that, based on the terms of the purchase of the employee's homes, the relocation management firm was in fact the new owner of the home. Therefore, under the terms of Revenue Ruling 82-204, the corporate taxpayer is not the owner of the home. Because of the structure of the transactions, the corporate taxpayer did not directly receive the gain or loss on the sales of the homes. In the final sentence of the ruling, the Internal Revenue Service stated that the employee's homes that were purchased under their agreements with the relocation management firms represented capital assets of the corporate taxpayer under Section 1221 of the Tax Code, and the amounts paid to the relocation firms are nondeductible capital expenditures that must be added to the bases of the homes.

In a Private Letter Ruling issued in August of 1992 (Private Letter Ruling 9244027), the Internal Revenue Service responded to a corporate taxpayer regarding the purchase of an employee's home. In this particular case, the corporate taxpayer was a limited partnership that provided relocation services to employers. As the relocation company explained their case, the relocation company entered into an agreement under which, upon notification of the intention of the corporation to move a transferee to another location, they would contact the employee to express its willingness to purchase the home. If the employee was agreeable, it would follow the normal process within the industry and obtain the opinion of value from two independent appraisers. The employee would select the appraisers from a list of qualified appraisers as offered by the relocation management firm. The value of the property would be calculated by averaging the appraisals. Once the value is calculated, the relocation firm would mail the offer to the employee who would have sixty days to try and market the home. If during this sixty-day period the employee was able to obtain a higher bona-fide offer, than the relocation company would match the offer creating an amended value transaction situation.

If the offer from the relocation firm is accepted, the employee will transfer to the relocation firm a good and marketable title to the property, executing a deed, and receiving payment of the equity in the home. Further, the relocation company stipulated that the treatment of such deed was in accordance with the requirements of state and local law regarding the acquisition of the title. Following the acceptance of the offer, the relocation company would take responsibility for the property after either the employee vacates the home or another sixty days has passed, whichever comes first. At that point the relocation company took the responsibility for all future expenses incurred in carrying, reselling, and closing the resale of the home.

The agreement between the relocation company and the employer stipulated that the employer will pay a fixed fee to the relocation company based upon a percentage the appraised value or the amended value of the home. The fixed fee is neither dependent nor affected by the costs incurred by the relocation company. The question before the Internal Revenue Service was whether the relocation firm was buying the homes for its own account or was it considered to be an agent of the employer.

In reviewing the facts of this situation and the various case law, the Internal Revenue Service ruled that the relocation company was purchasing the homes for their own account. This was based on the condition that the amount of the fee paid to the relocation company by the employer is determined through arm's length negotiation by the parties.

Four months later, in December, the Internal Revenue Service released Private Letter Ruling 9313015, which dealt once again with the income tax and employment tax requirements of relocation expenses made to the employee and the reporting requirements of those payments. According to the text of the Revenue Ruling, the corporate taxpayer maintains a relocation program under which it pays the relocation expenses of transferred employees and newly hired employees. The program allows for the reimbursement of the costs for house hunting, packing and transportation of household goods, the final trip , interim living expenses, and expenses related to the sale of the old residence. The corporate taxpayer also reimburses the employee for the estimated tax liability of the reimbursements for relocating.

The reason for the request to the Internal Revenue Service was that the corporate taxpayer had recently revised its relocation program for management employees in an effort to reduce the costs of the program and to encourage employees to reduce reimbursable moving expenses in the future. Under the new program, the corporate taxpayer imposed an individually calculated maximum limit upon any relocated employee's total reimbursed moving expense. The total cost of the move is estimated by looking at costs incurred by employees with similar move requirements and similar sized families. The costs are then reduced by ten to twenty percent as a cost-cutting factor. This reduced amount is then the relocation benefit that the employee will receive for the move.

Following the signing of a lump sum allowance advance agreement, the corporate taxpayer paid the employee the amount of the relocation expense amount calculated above. This agreement provides that the lump sum relocation allowance will be paid in conjunction with the employee's move. It further stipulates that if the employee voluntarily terminates his or her employment within two years after the transfer for which the allowance was paid or if the employee fails to purchase a new residence before a date specified in the individual's contract, the employee must repay the corporate taxpayer the amount of the lump sum payment with no interest being charged.

As required under the Tax Code, the employee agreed to provide the corporate taxpayer with a full accounting of the relocation expenses within ninety days of the move. Following the review of the expense report, the employee will pay to his employer who will pay the Internal Revenue Service any required federal withholding.

To encourage cost reductions in relocation situations, the corporate taxpayer agreed to pay the employee a relocation bonus in the amount by which the maximum reimbursable amount exceeds the total actual moving expenses.

The corporate taxpayer requested a ruling from the Internal Revenue Service on five issues arising out of the above-described program. First, the corporate taxpayer wanted to know when are the payments of the relocation allowances deemed received by the employee. Second, with the addition of relocation bonuses, the corporate taxpayer wanted to know when the bonuses are includible as gross income to the employee. Third, the corporate taxpayer wanted to know when and to what extent the relocation expense payments were subject to federal employment taxes. Fourth, the corporate taxpayer wanted to know whether the use of Form 4782 constituted a payee statement within the context of the Tax Code. Fifth, the corporate taxpayer wanted to know what the tax consequences were of the payback which was repaid in the same year as the allowance was given. Finally, the corporate taxpayer wanted to know the tax consequences of the payback being done in a subsequent year from when it was provided.

The Internal Revenue Service, after review of the issues in this case, issued this Private Letter Ruling with the following findings.

In regards to the first two questions, the Internal Revenue Service found that if the corporate taxpayer's advance or loan is calculated to

The Accountability Rule states that a relocating employee must account for actual expenses within a reasonable time. Further, the employee returns any excess of advances over expenses to his or her employer, and the employee does not take a deduction for these expenses but is still entitled to the standard deduction or other itemized deductions. The concept of *reasonable time* is rather vague at best. However, Section 1.62-2(g)(1) of the Internal Revenue Code states that a reasonable time will depend on the facts and circumstances surrounding the relocation. Section 1.62-2(g)(2) of the Internal Revenue Code states that substantiation furnished within sixty days or excess reimbursements returned within one hundred twenty days will be considered reasonable. In Private Letter Ruling 9313015, the Internal Revenue Service stated that ninety days

pay for the reasonably anticipated moving expenses, and the employee accounts for such expenses within a reasonable time, the employee is not deemed to have received a reimbursement of the moving expenses until the employee accounts to this employer. Further, the ruling stated that the provision of a relocation bonus exceeds the amount of the accounted expenses and so becomes income to the employee at the time of the accounting to the corporate taxpayer. An alternative suggested by the Internal Revenue Service was that, if the corporate taxpayer advance is in excess of the reasonably anticipated employee moving expenses, the employee must include in gross income the amount that exceeds the estimate of moving expenses. This income is deemed to have been paid at the point of accounting to the corporate taxpayer. The corporate taxpayer is entitled to deduct a reasonable advance as compensation when the employee accounts to his employer.

Looking at question three – concerning the taxability of relocation expenses – the Internal Revenue Service found that the moving expense reimbursements paid under the relocation program are wages for the purpose of withholding only at the time they are actually received by the employee and only to the extent that such payments exceed the amount believed to be reasonably deducted under the provisions of Section 217 of the Tax Code. The Internal Revenue Service also expressed the opinion that the relocation bonus was in fact income to the employee.

Prior to the latest changes in the Internal Revenue Code, the corporate taxpayer was required to provide the employee at the end of the year a copy of Form 4782 which provided the taxpayer with a record of all the relocation expenses incurred and which ones were considered to be taxable. The Internal Revenue Service stated that the Form was in fact a payee statement of the costs incurred in the move.

The final two issues that the Internal Revenue Service considered in this ruling dealt with the handling of the payback payments under the lump sum advance agreement that was signed between the employee and the corporate taxpayer. The Internal Revenue Service found that, if the repayment of the moving expense occurs in the same year as the initial payment, such allowance is not considered income to the employee. If on the other hand, the repayment occurs in a subsequent year, then the expense allowance is considered income for the purposes of federal withholding on income only. The deductions for FICA and FUTA are not wage considerations in this scenario.

A year later, the Internal Revenue Service would issue Private Letter Ruling 93-86 (1993-2 C.B. 71) that would have a profound effect on global relocations for the foreseeable future. The Tax Code had always had the policy that long term assignments were treated differently than short term assignments, but this became the first time that the Internal Revenue Service clarified what the difference was between the two assignment types. As stated above, this ruling clarified the terms of assignments. The issue presented in the ruling was what effect does the one-year limitation on temporary travel have on the deductibility of away from home travel expenses. In issuing its ruling, the Internal Revenue Service looked at three scenarios to express its views on this topic.

In the first scenario, the taxpayer is regularly employed in a city. In 1993 the taxpayer accepted work in another city that was two hundred fifty miles away from home. The taxpayer reasonably expected to work on site in the new location for six months and then planned on returning to his home. In fact, the employment contract lasted for ten months after which he returned home.

In the second scenario, the same facts were presented except the taxpayer in this case expected the work to last for eighteen months. After a time period of ten months, the project was completed and the employee returned home.

In the final scenario, the facts are the same as in the two previous scenarios except that the employee expected that the project would be completed in nine months. After a period of eight months it was determined that the project would actually take seven months more, for a total of fifteen months before returning home.

Section 162(a)(2) of the Tax Code states that in order for travel expenses to be deductible, they must be ordinary and necessary, they must be incurred while away from home, and they must be incurred in pursuit of a trade or business. The home, for the purpose of the Tax Code, is considered to be the taxpayer's regular of principal place of business.

The Revenue Ruling notes that an assignment that was planned to be temporary can change in nature due changed circumstances. Referring to Revenue Ruling 83-82, the Internal Revenue Service found that, if the taxpayer anticipates employment away from home to last less than one year, then all the facts and circumstances consider this assignment to be temporary in nature. If it extends beyond one year, then the assignment is considered to be indefinite. The ruling went on to state that, if the as-

is a reasonable period in which to account for moving expense advances per Section 82 of the Internal Revenue Code.

signment is realistically expected to last for one year or less, then the employment will be treated as a temporary assignment. If the assignment is realistically expected to last for one year or more, then it is considered to be indefinite in nature. The issue is when the assignment is expected to last for one year or less but turns into an indefinite assignment. The treatment then changes. The Internal Revenue Service ruled that the assignment will be considered a temporary assignment until such time as its duration of that assignment realistically changes. From that point on, it is considered to be an indefinite assignment. In the case under discussion, the Internal Revenue Service ruled that in scenario two above, the duration of the assignment was such that it expected to be an indefinite assignment. The fact that it ended in less than one year does not change the expectation of the length of the assignment.

In the third scenario, the employee went on the assignment expecting it to last for nine months. However, as things do happen in business, the circumstances changed to the point that it ended up lasting for over one year. Based on existing tax code, the assignment is considered temporary for the eight months, and thus the travel expenses that are paid or incurred are deductible. After the eight months, the assignment changes to an indefinite one, and the travel costs are not considered travel away from home and, therefore, are not deductible for the remaining seven months.

In July of 1994, a field agent, who was reviewing a corporate taxpayer's relocation program, again approached the Internal Revenue Service's National Office. The national office's review resulted in the issuance of Technical Advice Memorandum 9447002. In this case, the corporate taxpayer had established an employee relocation program, which was designed to assist the employees being transferred to new work locations. In essence, the program followed the same procedures as we have talked about earlier. The relocation management company ordered two independent appraisals that are averaged to arrive at the appraised value of the home. The employee was offered a forty-five-day window in which to try and beat the corporate offer. If the employee accepts the offer, the transferee would execute a deed and the contract offer and is given sixty days to vacate the property. Once the home is vacated, the property rights of the residence transfer to the relocation management firm. The question from the field agent was whether or not the employee realized compensation as the result of the amounts paid or incurred by the relocation management firm after it acquired possession of the property. After reviewing the terms of Section 1.82-1(a)(3) and Revenue Ruling 72-339, the national office determined that the amounts paid or incurred by the relocation management firm in connection with its sale of the transferee's residence are not included in the employee's gross income.

A little over a year later, in September of 1995, the Internal Revenue Service issued Private Letter Ruling 9552040. The ruling was in response to a request from PHH Homequity to clarify the terms of Revenue Ruling 72-339 as they pertain to the sale of a home by a transferee to a relocation management company, and would it give rise to income for the transferee for the commission that was neither paid nor incurred.

In the facts presented to the Internal Revenue Service, PHH Homequity stated that, among other services, it purchased and resold the homes of employees being relocated by their employers. PHH Homequity went on to explain that the process involved in the purchase of the property is one that is standard for the industry. Further, PHH Homequity stated that the employer reimburses the relocation firm for the expenses of the property. Another aspect of this set of facts is that PHH Homequity had provided the data from the purchase of over thirty-five thousand homes and had reached the conclusion that the Broker's Market Analysis (BMA) was as accurate in the long run as the appraisals, and that it would save the corporate clients both time and money if the BMA were the only values ordered.

The response by the Internal Revenue Service stated that if the employer or a relocation company hired by the employer purchases a relocating employee's home at fair market value under the circumstances described in Revenue Ruling 72-339, the employee must account for any gain on sale, but no compensation income is received. The Internal Revenue Service went on to state that based on the facts presented, the sale by an employee to the relocation management firm at fair market value will not give rise to income from compensation for the amount of a real estate commission that was neither paid nor incurred. The only area of the facts that the Internal Revenue Serviced refused to rule on was the method in which the fair market value was determined.

In the beginning of 1996, the Internal Revenue Service again visited this area when they issued Private Letter Ruling 9620026. This ruling took the prior issue one step further and asked the Internal Revenue Service to review whether the employee would realize gross income as the result of certain amounts paid or incurred by a relocation management in connection with its ownership and resale of the employee's personal residences. In their presentation to the Internal Revenue Service, the relocation management firm indicated that following the acceptance of the offer to purchase and the vacating of the property by the transferee, the relocation management firm assumes the beneficial title to the property. This meant that they assumed all the costs of owning the property including the maintenance and upkeep of the home. The question that was asked was whether under the terms of Section 82 of the Tax Code these expenditures meant that the employee realized income for the amounts spent.

In reviewing the facts in this request, the Internal Revenue Service found that the amounts paid or incurred were items which benefited either the relocation management firm or the corporate taxpayer. The costs were imposed on these entities after the employee relinquished the rights and benefits of ownership of the property. Therefore, the costs are not considered income to the transferee.

In June of 1977, the US Tax Court entered the relocation picture when it rendered its opinion in a case called *Amdahl Corporation v. Commissioner of the Internal Revenue Service.* In order to better understand the impact that this case would have on relocation, let's begin with some background on the corporation.

The Amdahl Corporation is a Delaware incorporated corporation with headquarters in Sunnyvale, California and was at the time in the business of developing, manufacturing, marketing, and servicing large-scale computer systems, storage products, communication systems, software, and educational services. Amdahl also supplied product and software support for the systems it sold as well as research, development, and consulting services. At the time of the case, Amdahl employed between sixty-six and seventy-two hundred employees worldwide with the vast majority based in the United States.

At issue in the case before the Tax Court was whether the payments made by Amdahl to the relocation management firms in order to assist in the disposition of the homes of its employees who were asked by Amdahl to relocate were deductible against ordinary income or must they be treated as a capital loss.

In the information provided to the Tax Court by Amdahl, the company indicated that they relocate both current and newly hired employees as its business needs dictate. The location of many of these relocations is to locations where it has installed mainframe computers to provide maintenance services to its customers. The corporation also stated that it relocates employees as it expands into new geographic markets to ensure that it has employees at the new location who are familiar with the company, its products, and its customers. In order to induce employees to relocate, Amdahl provided various kinds of employee benefits to assist in the move. These benefits included household goods shipments, house-hunting trips, shipment of personal effects, household pets relocation, movement of family vehicles, final trip expenses, temporary living, return trips if needed, and tax liability protection.

As part of this program, Amdahl offered to its employees financial assistance in the sale of their current residence as the result of the relocation. The corporation had done so for the previous twenty years. In order to achieve this goal, Amdahl has contracted with three unrelated corporations to provide the service. In completion of the terms of the agreement, the relocation management firm offers to purchase and resell the residences of the eligible Amdahl employees. The costs involved with the program are billed to Amdahl, who in turn reimburses those costs back to the relocation management firm. The relocation management firm agrees to purchase the residences at fair market value, which is based on the average of two independent appraisals. Copies of all appraisals are sent to Amdahl Corporation, and the offer is contingent on acceptance within sixty days from receipt.

At the time of the acceptance of the offer from Amdahl, the employee signs and delivers a deed-in-blank to the relocation management firm. This deed-in-blank is not recorded. The deed-in-blank is held until such time as there is an outside purchaser for the home. The employee maintains legal title to the property until the ultimate sale of the residence. At this time, the employee is given sixty days to vacate the property. After their vacating the property, the relocation management firm assumes all the burdens and benefits of ownership. Generally, the net sale proceeds to Amdahl Corporation following the closing with the outside buyer. In turn, Amdahl reimburses the relocation management firm for the equity payments and all the costs the relocation management firm incurred in connection with the disposition of the residence. The contract with the relocation management firm also included a service fee based on a set percentage of the appraised value.

Amdahl further stated in their information that they never intended to assume title to the property, and, therefore, it viewed the costs associated with assisting the relocating employees as an expense of conducting its computer business and did not intend to profit from the sales of the residence to a third party.

In it's ruling the Tax Court found that several issues played a role here. First was the question of whether, as the Internal Revenue Service claimed, Amdahl had taken title to the property and was now the rightful owner of the property. Based on several different Tax Court cases, the Court ruled that the economic substance of the transaction controls the determination as to whether the transaction constitutes a sale for Federal tax purposes. Under Federal codes, the sale occurs upon the transfer of benefits and burdens of ownership. The Tax Court went on to state that Amdahl did not acquire legal ownership of the residences in question. The second part of the equation was that due to language in the Amdahl Relocation Information package, the Internal Revenue Service claimed that the relocation management firms were acting as an agent of the seller. The Tax Court found no such evidence. However, they also found that the relocation management firm did not acquire beneficial ownership of the property, either.

In another issue, the Internal Revenue Service claimed that the contract for sale between the relocation management firm and the employee were in fact binding contracts for sale. The court refuted this. The Internal Revenue Service further stated that the relocation management company equity payments were such as to give them equity interest in the homes. Again, the Tax Court disagreed.

There were several other issues that were considered, but in summary, the Tax Court found that Amdahl did not acquire beneficial ownership of the residences. This was based on the fact that all the supporting documents indicated that the employee retained the benefits and burdens of ownership until the home was eventually sold. Having found that Amdahl was not the owner of the homes, the Tax Court decided that Amdahl was entitled to deduct the payments to the relocation management firm as ordinary and necessary business expenses.

While many of the events discussed above had an effect on the relocation process, the industry underwent its own internal changes. In order to bring some professionalism to the industry, the Employee Relocation Council introduced, the Certified Relocation Professional™ designation program in 1990. The purpose of the program was to establish one body of knowledge that relocation professionals would know and understand. This was accomplished by the publication of a series of books and *Mobility Magazine* articles which talked about the trends within the industry.

Another aspect of the changing industry was a change in the delivery model. Immense layoffs occurred in the 1980's. IBM continued the process in the early days of this decade with the elimination of twenty-five thousand jobs worldwide. The result was more and more companies began to consider the process of outsourcing all non-functional aspects of the company to an outside provider. While the partial outsourcing of relocation had been going on since the time when our journey began, it was more prevalent now than ever before. This created a new animal in the marketplace called the *Human Resource Organization* or *Personnel Employment Organization*. Their impact will be discussed more in depth in part 4 of this book.

With all this going on, we also saw the beginning of seventeen new companies entering the field and several more mergers among the players including PHH Homequity purchasing Better Homes and Gardens Relocation.

7
NEW
MILLENNIUM
(2000 – 2004)

There is a saying in the feminist movement, "We've come a long way, baby!" The same can be said for the journey we have undertaken. Over the previous chapters I have taken you on a journey from the days when the concept of providing relocation services to transferees was pie-in-the-sky to the days when it became a real, viable part of the recruiting packages of many corporations.

We have now reviewed the past and the present perspectives of the journey through corporate relocation. This chapter looks not at a full decade but rather only the past four years. This period has seen a dramatic change in the relocation industry due to a myriad of reasons. Each of these forces has changed the world we live in, the world we work in, and the way corporations look at the whole concept of relocation services.

In 2000, the industry was faced with yet another issue. In the State of Florida, there is, in essence, a bounty-hunter clause in the state revenue code. It states that if an entity is able to recover monies that are due to the state, then those entities are entitled to a percentage of that amount recovered as a bounty for obtaining the state funds that were not paid. A group of lawyers led by Roy Oppenheim, who was a well connected attorney from West Palm Beach, Florida, operating under the name *Private AG*, sued several of the major relocation companies in Florida. The suit alleged that by using a deed-in-blank, the relocation companies had deprived the State of Florida coffers of millions of dollars since 1992. The suit was filed despite the Director of Revenue and the Attorney General stating that there was no case. Eventually, the case was thrown out of court. The aftereffect of this lawsuit combined with the various decisions laid down by both the Tax Court and the Commissioner of the Internal Revenue Service put the industry on notice. The direct result of these decisions was that the Policy and Practices Committee of the Employee Relocation Council advocated that all parties involved in the relocation process should issue two deeds in any home purchase transaction.

Let me back track a little and explain the differences between the two scenarios. Up until this time, the standard practice in the industry was for the transferee to accept the corporate offer by signing the offer and a deed in which the purchaser's name was left blank until the ultimate sale to the outside purchaser. This had been the practice since the industry began in the 1950's. The change called for the transferee to now place the name of the corporation or the relocation management company in the space for the purchaser when they sold the home to the corporation. The relocation management company then would create a new deed for the sale between the relocation management company and the ultimate purchaser. While this created more paperwork and potentially higher fees, it was felt by the Employee Relocation Council that this was more in line with the conditions that the Internal Revenue Service had laid out for the creation of two separate and distinct transactions in any home purchase scenario.

In addition, the new century ushered in a time when many corporations decided that greed was more important than taking care of the human capital within their organizations. It was the era during which corporate greed appeared on our front pages of the morning newspaper in the form of the scandals at Enron and Tyco. This greed would result in outsourcing of both the relocation function and the human resource functions.

This greed and the resulting scandals would see the introduction and passage of the Sarbanes-Oxley Act. Section 402 of this act had a particular impact on the relocation industry. It had been common to offer transferees a bridge loan to cover the costs of purchasing a new home prior to the sale of the old home. The bridge loan was contingent on service on the job for a specified period of time and was repayable on the closing of the old residence. Section 402 of the Sarbanes-Oxley Act stated that from the point of enactment, it became unlawful for any public company to extend or maintain credit, or arrange for the extension of credit, in the form of a personal loan to or for any director or executive officer (or the equivalent thereof) either directly or indirectly. The Act made no exceptions for the bridge loans in a relocation situation. At first, many observers believed that this would create a major problem for our industry. In retrospect, over the years since its passage, most people that I have talked with indicate that it is a non-issue in many relocation situations.

The largest impact on the relocation industry occurred on September 11, 2001 with the terrorist attack on the Pentagon, the World Trade Center, and a field in Pennsylvania. In a matter of seconds, the whole nature of the relocation industry changed along with the entire rest of the business community. The effects on the relocation industry, in particular, were substantial in nature. For many years many of my fellow relocation peers and I told everyone that relocation was recession proof. No matter what the condition of the economy, corporations had to move people in order to keep their operations functioning. No matter what, our jobs were secure because what we provided was a necessity for the completion of a successful relocation for the transferee and the corporation. That all changed on that day in mid-September. The industry, as a result, suffered its first ever downturn in volume. Corporations were second-guessing relocations that might have been planned. Individuals were reconsidering the acceptance of relocations. In some cases the view was that relocation to a remotely placed suburb was, in the long run, safer than living near the big cities.

Additionally, corporations began to look at the deliverance of relocation services as a commodity. Instead of looking at the impact of the relocation on the productivity of the employee or the impact on the human capital talent, the perspective changed to look at, Let's see how cheap we can get the services delivered. One Fortune 1000 corporation even went so far as to title the individual responsible for relocation as *Commodity Manager Relocation*. Also, responsibility for the selection of relocation services vendors shifted from Human Resources to the Purchasing Department.

The impact of this shift has become very important for the development of the industry within the last four years. I guess you could say that, like everything else in the business world, things move in cycles. When the industry began, it was commonplace for the vendor selections to be made by the traffic department, which did so in conjunction with the purchasing department. The drawback to this approach is that the decisions are made purely from a financial perspective. The transferee becomes an afterthought in the view of the corporation. The other difficulty with purchasing being involved in the process is that it does not understand the impact of its decisions on the corporate human capital. Every decision is made based on the bottom line, not what is best for the employee. The impact gets carried through to the vendor because with smaller profit margins for their services, they must collect the difference somewhere. That somewhere becomes the vendors that the relocation management company must use to fulfill its end of the commitment. This means that the real estate brokers and others are asked to fork over higher referral commission rates to compensate for the gap.

A direct result of this change of approach was that once the corporate orientation switched from the employee to the bottom line, the quality of service declined. This decline resulted in the employee being, more or less, left alone to solve the problems of relocation. This decline came in the middle of a recession and the nature of relocations changing. Corporations began to maintain only bare bone staff in-house. This meant that the employees were forced to rely on outsiders for the answers to their questions – if they could find anyone with the requisite knowledge. As a result, the individual became very much cost sensitive when relocations were offered. One reason for this sensitivity was corporations began to guarantee fewer home buyouts, instead pushing the employee towards what became known as *buyer value option*. Under this program the corporation could save money by not providing appraisals, instead depending on the free market to determine what the value of the property was.

This turn to buyer value options was just one sign of the change in the view of corporations towards relocation. This move to a bottom line view of benefits resulted in program cutbacks not just in home purchase but also in other aspects of the relocation process. Instead of paying large amounts for the purchase of homes, the corporations returned to an earlier period by re-instituting lump sum payments to transferees. In essence, the corporation told the employee that in return for accepting a new position, they would provide the transferee with a set amount of funds to cover the relocation expenses. Whatever the employee did not spend became their signing bonus for accepting the position.

This shifting viewpoint also resulted in a change in how the relocation process was handled. First, the outsourcing of the relocation function led to the relocation management company becoming the gatekeeper of the process. This meant that if a particular vendor wanted to do business with a particular corporation, the vendor needed to be approved by the third-party company rather than the internal department. The relocation company, therefore, charged a fee for access to the system. The relocation companies used these fees as a prequel for the establishment of the service charges to their corporate clients. The case presented by the relocation management firms stated that they could keep the fees down to the corporation through the collection of referral fees from the vendors in the process. These vendors, among others, included real estate agents and household goods companies.

As the new century opened, we also found the economy changing. Following the Clinton presidency, the country underwent a recession and the burst of the high-tech bubble, which developed in the 1990's. The dotcoms underwent a period of rapid growth followed by a rapid decline. This rapid decline resulted in a large number of positions either being eliminated or sent overseas where the corporations could find people at half of the annual salary to perform the same job duties.

One solution to these changes was a greater dependence on technology. This change in technology resulted in new alternatives to delivering not only relocation but all aspects of human resources to the human capital component of the corporation. The result was that intranet sites were developed which allowed the employee to obtain the information they needed twenty-four hours a day, seven days a week. This information was constructed in such a way that the employee could go to the site and get direct real-time information regarding what benefits they were entitled to, the ability to file expense reports, and e-mail the correct contact person who could solve the problem.

The final aspect of our look at the past four years turns to the Internal Revenue Service who, once again, decided to look at the whole relocation process. Following the decisions in Amdahl, the various Published Revenue Rulings and the vast array of Private Letter Rulings, the government again began to look at whether the home sale transaction was actually two distinct transactions. They also were interested in whether the costs of such programs were documented to show what was actually proper business expenses. In those cases where the argument could not be clearly shown, the Internal Revenue Service began to seek compensation for deductions given but not legitimately done so.

These past four years have been dramatic for the relocation industry. However, as we will see in the last part of this book, the rest of this decade, and even the rest of the century, could very well have a huge impact on how we treat the human capital talent in our workplace. But before we get to that point, we will first look at another aspect of the relocation process – the development of the relocation department within the real estate brokerage.

8

CASE STUDY: AT&T

In the introduction, I made reference to the fact that one of the audiences for this book was the new relocation professional. The individual who knows only that say, in order to enter into a home purchase program, you need to get two appraisals, simply because that is just the way it is. As the journey reached the present, I looked for a way to try summarizing the history of the relocation industry in a fashion which would clearly show where we have been. In looking at the first section of this book, I came to realize that there was no greater impact on the industry that we call home than the efforts by the people at American Telephone and Telegraph. In reviewing the history of American Telephone and Telegraph, the company has a well established record of creating firsts within the corporate world within the United States. This was true whether we were talking about the creation of transistors which ran many of our telephonic and electronic industries to the creation of UNIX. The corporation's involvement in the relocation industry is no less impressive. It was their efforts, innovations, and foresight that pushed the industry to the point where it is today. What was interesting to me was that as I talked to some of the elders of the industry, the response often heard was, "Oh, so that is why we did that."

As I began the research for the preparation of this case study, I had the privilege to talk with the individuals who were there as it happened. I need to thank Bob Ilsley (1946-1988), Mauro Fanelli (1955-1987), Vinnie Riccoli (1970-1984), Julian Dorf (1978-1983), Peter Klein (1960-1989), and John Bemont (1963-1998). Their time and insight into the impact of their efforts on the relocation industry were invaluable in the writing of the case study.

As far as the relocation innovations of the company are concerned, it is not necessary to go back to the beginning of the corporation. The innovations in relocation can be traced back to the era after World War II. In 1946, an executive within the human resources function approached a young man who had recently left the military and was working in the accounting department of the firm. The human resource executive asked this individual whether he would be interested in working in relocation for American Telephone and Telegraph. Bob Ilsley's response was, "Working in what?" Neither he nor his new boss was exactly sure what relocation was.

When Bob Ilsley made the transition over to human resources, there was not even a basic policy in place. In fact, the company was moving

In 1990, American Telephone and Telegraph outsourced their relocation program. When we asked for input from both AON, the outsource company, and from Public Relations of American Telephone and Telegraph – out of concern for the AT&T brand name –the decision was made not to provide the information for the last fourteen years of the corporate relocation program. The years in parentheses represent the years in which the individuals worked for the Bell System.

American Telephone and Telegraph consisted of a group of companies including Long Lines, Western Electric, Southern Bell, South Central Bell, Southwestern Bell, Pacific Bell, Nevada Bell, Illinois Bell, Indiana Bell, Michigan Bell, Ohio Bell, Wisconsin Bell, Northwestern Bell, Diamond State Bell, Chesapeake Bell, New Jersey Bell, New York Telephone, New England Telephone, Mountain States Bell and Bell Labs. The individual state Bell Companies earned the nickname of the Baby Bells, which even though the company has been broken up, has remained in place to the present day.

people with no policy at all. As a result the first project that was undertaken was to write a policy. This began the era of innovation in relocation, as it was possibly the first relocation policy written by any corporation in the country. At the time, American Telephone and Telegraph operations consisted of the General department, which was corporate headquarters, and over twenty subsidiary operating companies. The first segment of the Bell System to receive the benefits of this new effort in relocation was the Long Lines Division, which was responsible for the long distance operations. If you were to speak with Bob Ilsley, he would tell you that admittedly in the early days they flew by the seat of their pants in trying to put the right mixture of policy components together since there were no benchmarks of policies in existence on which they could model the new effort.

The policy design effort began by looking at who was being relocated and was eligible for the benefits under the new policies. It was immediately determined that the crafts areas of the employment base (e.g., linesman) would not be included in the program. Part of the thinking was that the new program was a benefit to the executives who were rotated in and out of headquarters. The policy components were also provided to women who were being asked to relocate at this time.

One group of executives was having a hard time under the program. This group of managers was in the lower levels of the management structure and, for the most part, the executives owned mobile homes. As you may be aware, the price of mobile homes continues to depreciate as they age which meant that they were difficult to enter into a home purchase program. The solution that AT&T developed was to take these mobile homes and place them on a cement block base and call them a home, which now made them eligible for the home purchase program. This model idea was carried on to the entire industry.

By 1955, when Mauro Fanelli began his career in relocation, the program was well in place. However, the program had two operational plans.

The first part of the plan was called the *Long Lines Program*. One of the characteristics of the Long Lines Operation was that there were no long-term employees, *per se*. The management of the division consisted of executives from the subsidiary companies who were normally rotated into Long Lines for a two-year stint and then returned to their original companies. The problem was that the program used two different relocation policies. One covered the move to corporate and was paid for by corporate.

The second was the move back to the subsidiary, and that move was paid for by the subsidiary. The difficulty was that the policies were sufficiently different that the employee typically lost out on the return move.

The Long Lines program provided the employee with a three-year mortgage differential, household goods movement, and sixty-days of storage in transit. It further stipulated that if the employee was moving less than three hundred miles from their original location, the employee was expected to return to the departure location each weekend. It was during the implementation of this program that American Telephone and Telegraph created an innovation that is common in the industry today. Requiring no documentation, American Telephone and Telegraph created a program to assist their employees that we now call a *lump sum allowance*. The company also provided the employee with funds to cover the tax ramifications by *grossing up* the salaries to cover these extra charges.

It was about this time, following the Homequity/Potere contract with Western Electric, that a memo was sent from the executive offices of American Telephone and Telegraph to all the subsidiary companies. This memo stated that the handling of the home purchase program could be better implemented if each subsidiary company sought out its own third-party management firm. The memo requested that the selection process be fully implemented by 1968. As a result, twenty relocation management firms were created just from the impact of this memo. The Long Lines Division itself utilized the services of Equitable, Franklin Capital, Merrill Lynch, and Homequity. American Telephone and Telegraph hired an internal individual to keep track of all the homes that came into inventory (i.e., homes bought by the company). The list of these available homes were provided to all internal transfers at a sixty percent discount off the appraised value.

Another aspect of this developing program was that the Long Lines Department was greatly concerned with the perception managers might have of the new area professionals. As a result the company developed a policy prohibiting the recommendation of a specific real estate agent in the new community. As we reached into the late 1970's and into the next decade, when interest rates began their dramatic climb, the corporation also informed the employees of the company that no relative of the employee could hold a valid real estate license. This was done in order to avoid the pressure for managers to refer the new manager to their spouses to assist in locating new residences. Prior to the introduction of tiered

From the research we have completed, these assignments created Van Schaack (Mountain Bell); Transequity (Northwestern Bell); Sherwood Roberts (Pacific Northwest Bell); Transamerica (Pacific Bell and Nevada Bell); Employee Transfer Corporation (Illinois Bell); Bank of St Louis (Southwestern Bell); Gilby Relocation(Michigan Bell); Equitable (New York Telephone); Homequity (Chesapeake and Potomoc).

policies, all the employees received the exact same policy benefits if they were asked to move by the company.

The second part of the plan, called the *Bedminister Plan*, involved those employees being moved only from New York to New Jersey and began about 1975. During the process the company moved three hundred fifty employees into Bedminster and three hundred fifty additional employees to Basking Ridge. For those employees who were asked to move across the Hudson River, the company provided them with a vast array of benefits. The employees were offered a car loan, reimbursement for driving and training, a five-year mortgage differential and tax reimbursement benefit, and an allowance to assist in finding a new home. Part of the home finding allowance program was that the company would provide a van which was used by groups of employees being transferred to Bedminster to get a tour of the new community. This area tour included the spouse to also see where they would spend the next several years. The benefit package also included a guarantee against loss on the sale of their old home and sixty days storage in transit.

The corporation also set up a network of eight attorneys to which these employees were referred to for the closing process in New Jersey. Part of this plan also established a negotiated fee for service that the employee could expect from the attorney they chose to assist with the closing of their new home purchase. Later, the same system was established for the household goods firms who wanted to obtain the AT&T business.

These two systems are the first examples we were able to verify that set the precedent of constructing a network of preferred vendors, which became common among the relocation management firms within the ensuing decade.

In dealing with the household goods firms, American Telephone and Telegraph began the process of taking the invoices from the moves and comparing them to the program benefits and the estimates for accuracy. Once again these systems would become prevalent throughout the industry over the next decade.

The final aspect of this program required the employee to get a letter of approval from his or her operating unit to move. This aspect of the program would come into play later in the history of the program.

By the end of the 1970's, the company decided to go outside the organization and hire a fresh face to handle the relocation program. At the time of Julian Dorf's arrival in 1978, the company's relocation program was spread over sixteen to eighteen relocation management firms and was different in each division of the company. One outcome of this situation was that the company had over two thousand inventoried homes at the time of Dorf's arrival with the company. Part of this was that corporate headquarters had abdicated any responsibility for the program and left the decisions on policy to the divisions.

Like Bob Ilsley when he started in the program, Julian Dorf was sent out on his own to bring the program under control. His initial efforts involved rewriting the contracts with the relocation management firms and reducing their numbers to a maximum of eight from eighteen. Under Dorf's guidance, the relocation policy was redesigned completely for the entire company – with the exception of Western Electric. Due to high interest rates at the time, the program carried forward the three-year Mortgage Interest Differential program for relocating employees with the potential for a descending scale on payments as the employee progressed further out from the inception of the mortgage program. This was designed to help compensate for the large differences in interest rates around the country.

One of the highlights of the Dorf era occurred in 1981. At that time American Telephone and Telegraph was moving about fifteen thousand employees per year. Dorf believed that there was a way to streamline the process and enhance its usefulness for all the parties involved. So the company approached Salomon Brothers who was one of the corporations investment banking sources. The idea was that a program would be introduced which would speed up the mortgage process for transferred employees.

The program was designed so that American and Telegraph would do all the administrative work up-front, such as completing the forms. They also produced a guidebook for the employee explaining the relocation process. In turn the employee was referred to Norwest Mortgage who conducted a half-hour to forty-five minute interview based on the information provided by the employer. Norwest would then approve the mortgage within a half hour of the interview and arrange for the closing. The mortgage, in turn, was given to Salomon Brothers who sold the mortgage as securities on the secondary mortgage market. On the very first day of the program's implementation, Salomon Brothers balked at the program and left the process. They would later recruit Julian Dorf away from AT&T.

The Secondary Mortgage Market consists of three primary semi-governmental agencies. They are the Government National Mortgage Association (GNMA), Federal Home Loan Mortgage Corporation (Freddie Mac) and the Federal National Mortgage Association (Fannie Mae). They each sell mortgages in the form of securities on the secondary market to finance loans for home

As the industry developed, a common practice was the creation of *affinity programs* where the relocation benefits were applied to all the corporate employees and not just to the relocating employee. In the mid-eighties, the relocation program of American Telephone and Telegraph created the industry's very first affinity program.

Following the departure of Julian Dorf, the corporation turned to one of their other divisions, Bell Labs, and asked Pete Klein to assume control over the relocation program. During Pete Klein's six-years tenure at control of the program, the policy was enhanced by using the services of Moran, Stahl, and Boyer to provide for the first time both home sale incentives and home marketing assistance. These new aspects of the relocation program were designed to help the employee make wise decisions about the sale of their home. It was also during this era that one of the members of upper management began questioning whether it would make more sense to outsource the function, but nothing ever became of it until almost ten years later. At the end of 1989, Pete Klein urged a co-worker to take over the position. This individual was John Bemont.

During John Bemont's era, many changes occurred in the relocation program. First, the policy was tightened up in the area of costs. The original relocation policy was delivered as an entitlement. The employee was being moved and expected these services. But the Bemont era changed this aspect of the program. The employee assumed part of the responsibility for the home sale program. It was still the same program. However, the employee participated in the marketing effort of the home. Part of the participation by the employee was the linking of the list price to the appraised value of the home. In most cases, the employee was expected to list the home within a certain range of its appraised value.

During the latter part of the 1980's, the lump sum program was expanded into a tiered plan based on the business unit to which the employee was assigned. The direct result was that exceptions and appeals were eliminated. Those individual units developed the individual plans with guidance from the corporate relocation department. One of the aspects that AT&T introduced at this time was to tell an employee that the relocation department would approve an exception to the relocation policy if the employee could get approval from the business unit that they worked for.

Another aspect of the relocation program changes was the development of groups of income characteristics. The company estimated the gross up level at the indicated income level. The employee was then paid the amount of the estimated gross up to compensate for the tax liabilities of the move. The primary objective of the lump sum program and the tax gross-up plan was to run a program with no exceptions to policy and save money in the long run.

It was at this time that an earlier concept reappeared on the AT&T scene. It began in 1986 when the list of relocation vendors was reduced to two – Prudential and Homequity. As time went on, more and more of the relocation function was turned over to these two relocation management firms. It was assumed that these two corporations, being experts in relocation, would do a better job than the internal staff. In 1990, the total program was outsourced to AON, who would run the total outsourced human resource function in the near future.

While this review of the relocation program over a period of some forty years is brief at best, it was not designed to be an all-encompassing look at relocation in the Bell world. What it was designed to do was to show how the American Telephone and Telegraph innovations in relocation over the years have carried over to the relocation community as a whole. The innovations such as lump sums, gross-up, and affinity programs have become a staple of virtually every relocation program in the country. AT&T was the basis for the development of these programs and refined and perfected perfect them as they were rolled out to the whole relocation community.

Part II

Find Me a Place to Live

The Role of the Real Estate Relocation Department

9
HISTORY
OF
THE
RELOCATION
DEPARTMENT

The corporation has reviewed its operations, and for whatever the reason, the decision has been made to ask an employee to uproot his or her family and lifestyle to relocate to another community for the good of the company. Take notice of the fact that we said *for the good of the company.* This is due to the fact that some relocations make no sense for the transferee, but due to economic conditions, they are forced to move anyway.

Either consciously or subconsciously, the first thought that comes into the mind of the employee and his or her family is *How do I duplicate my current lifestyle in this new community I am being asked to relocate to?* The key to finding the answer to this question is the input from seasoned professionals who know the community. In most cases the entity that is turned to is the local real estate broker. The key contact in these real estate broker operations has been and should be the relocation departments. The question before the broker is *What level of assistance do I deliver to the transferee?* The following two chapters will examine the answers to that question. Chapter 9 looks at the development of the relocation departments within the broker community from a historical perspective. Chapter 10 on the other hand looks at the relocation departments and how they are coping with the new business model being imposed on the industry.

Looking back at the history of the real estate profession, we find that the first individuals to call themselves *real estate brokers* came about the same time as Samuel Carter and Reuben Washburn made their trek to San Francisco for Wells Fargo. These real estate brokers would go out in advance of the railroad and stage lines for the purpose of securing property as these companies began their development westward. The relocation departments within these brokerages would not come into existence until the latter part of the twentieth century. Like the third-party relocation management firms discussed in Part One of this book, the relocation departments were not the result of some grandiose plan with a lot of foresight. Instead, they were the response to the needs of a particular situation at a given time in the journey. The first impetus for the creation of relocation departments came about with the creation of Homerica and the American Family Relocation Service. These departments were the direct result of the request for assistance from the earliest of the referral groups which would soon follow.

As was stated in Chapter 1, Don McPherson accepted a move from Chicago to New York in 1955. In the process of making the move, McPher-

See the reference to Samuel Carter and Reuben Washburn on Page 21 of this work. They represented the beginning of financial people moving westward to the gold mines from the east coast at the request of Wells Fargo.

son looked at no less than seventy-five communities before finally settling in southern Connecticut around New Canaan. McPherson's experiences reflected the characteristics of the times. First, it was evidence of a belief among the corporations that there place was to stay out of the personal lives of their employees. The direct result was that when employees were asked to make a move they were essentially on their own. The second piece of evidence was that this era was prior to the introduction of the *Multiple Listing Services* (MLS). It therefore meant that if an employee wanted to look at twenty different homes in a community, they needed to contact twenty different brokers to see the homes they wanted to see. This was because there was no such thing as a cooperating broker in the real estate process.

McPherson was determined that this situation would not repeat itself with other transferees being asked to move. While its purpose was not real estate oriented, the Homerica program developed a system under which the employee would be thoroughly counseled on the new areas they were contemplating relocating to. Starting with the New York Metropolitan area and then spreading out to the major metropolitan areas of the country, each transferee worked directly with a trained counselor who helped them assess the pros and cons of the new community. Following the completion of the counseling process, the transferee was referred to a broker chosen by Homerica to assist in finding a residence in that community. In the beginning, Homerica worked with about twenty brokers in the New York area, and that number increased to about two hundred when it spread across the country prior to becoming Homequity. This system became the business model for the brokerage community and the third party companies, which would follow in the future.

It would take almost another decade (seven years to be exact) before the real estate companies began the process of starting internal departments to deal with the relocating transferee. Prior to the creation of these departments, the norm for the assignment of these leads followed a rather set policy. As the transferee called into the office asking for assistance, they were often turned over to the office secretary or receptionist. In turn, this individual assigned the lead to one of three types of individuals.

The first scenario was that the broker or his designated employee assigned the lead to the agent who just happened to be in the office at the time. The agent then proceeded to work the lead, whether or not they knew the area or understood how a relocation lead was different from the other leads coming into the office. Further, from a personality perspective, it did not matter whether the agent could work effectively with the transferee.

The second scenario is one in which the broker assigned the lead to the top-producing agent in the office. The belief was that the top producers were the individuals within the office with the best knowledge of the area. The drawback was that the exceptionally busy agent might not have the time to adequately provide the kind of hand holding that relocation required.

The third scenario was that some brokers used the relocation leads as an incentive or reward for the agent who was in a slump to try and get them back on top of their game. Once again, the flaw in this process was that the agent might not have been the right match for the transferee.

This idea began to change in 1962, when a broker in Tulsa, Oklahoma began the process of establishing an in-house relocation department. In this year, Deep Rock Petroleum made the decision to move its operations from Tulsa to Denver. Based on the apparent need, Sheldon Detrick began the process by utilizing the services of one of his sales agents, Betsy York. Ms. York was a gregarious person who had a genuine need to assist people and was not concerned with the commission aspect of the process. As part of the services rendered by Detrick Realty, the transferees were referred to Poly Little Realty in Denver who provided the destination services end of the move for the Deep Rock Petroleum employees and their families.

Sheldon Detrick was the broker-owner of Detrick Realty. Sheldon is still the broker of record of the agency, which now operates as Prudential Detrick/Alliance Realty.

Five years later, in 1967, Detrick Realty formalized the relocation department process by choosing to make Betsy York a full-time employee and paying her a salary instead of commission. The department in turn would generate the leads for the agents with a charge to the agents of a fifteen percent referral fee. The fee was generated on the premise that when the transferee had been turned over to an agent in the office, they had already completed the area counseling process with the Relocation Department. Part of this counseling process included ascertaining the type of individual that the transferee liked working with. For instance, was the transferee most comfortable working with a female agent or someone who had been around awhile? This meant that valuable time was saved on the part of the agent who did not have to pre-sell the area before locating properties since this was done ahead of time.

The total evolutionary period of the relocation departments ran from 1955 to the end of the 1980's. But by the early 1960's, many of the larger brokers across the United States had begun to move in the direction of establishing such departments. As stated earlier the operations ran from the office secretary handling calls to the leads going to the highest producing agents in the company. The logic behind this method of handling leads was that relocation was new and an ancillary service that some brokers felt like trying out to see if it would work.

The founding members of the "Dirty Dozen" were Moore and Company (Denver, CO), F.C. Tucker Company (Indianapolis, IN), West Shell Realty (Cincinnati, OH), Real Estate One (Cleveland, MN), GSH Real Estate (Virginia Beach, VA), HER Realtors (Columbus, OH), Hooten Stahl Realtors (Albuquerque, NM), Henry S Miller (Dallas, TX), Howard Hanna Company (Pittsburgh, PA), Patterson-Schwartz (Hockessin, DE) and Norwood Realty (Bedford, NH), Wauwatosa Realty (Wauwatosa, MN), Stan Wiley Real Estate (Portland, OR). Later another group called the Masterminds also started. Eventually the two groups combined into what today is known as the Realty Alliance.

One of the telltale characteristics was the attitude of the broker who owned the real estate firm. If we surveyed the brokers at the time, they could be divided into two separate groups. The first group was the broker who let his ego get in the way. This was characterized by the broker who never understood what relocation was all about nor cared to learn. They were the brokers who added a relocation department because it was the thing to do. There was even a real estate broker I worked with in the 1990's who asked me, "How many dollars per square foot does the relocation department generate for the brokerage?" These brokers did not understand the full nature of the relocation operations in the long run for the bottom line. For example, they did not understand that if the transferee's needs were met, then when they were ready to move again, the transferee was very likely to go back to the same agent.

The other side of the picture was represented by brokers such as Wes Foster (Long and Foster Realty), Chip Roach (Prudential Fox-Roach), Sheldon Detrick, and others who truly saw what this new avenue of business could mean for the company. Some of their early beginnings came out of meetings with other brokers across the country that had similar ideas of where the real estate industry was headed. Following a meeting in 1971, a number of brokers of this mindset created a group, who called themselves the *Dozen*. They were not relocation oriented *per se*, but relocation became a topic that was discussed. Many of these brokers went on to lead some of the leading relocation brokerages in the industry.

The remainder of this chapter will look at the development of the relocation programs within these more forward-thinking brokers. The reader must first understand the environment in which we were operating. Following the 1960's, the level of relocation business began to increase dramatically as was discussed earlier. However, the relocation industry was not working as a cohesive service. The brokerages usually began the process by asking the office administrator or the office receptionist to be the initial contact for the leads that were coming into the office. As we entered the 1960's, many of the brokers began to form regional and national referral networks to capture the intercity home finding and home sale business. They also wanted to try and capture this new area of business. Part of entering these referral networks required that the structure of the brokerages needed to change. The result was that the brokerage firm now began to look for the right individual to become a referral coordinator.

These referral coordinators were full-time individuals who were paid a salary and who accepted the responsibility for handling the referrals coming into the firm. Their duties included getting the transferee newcomer information and providing some idea about the community to the transferee and the family. The referral coordinator was not concerned about the administration of relocation policies or the requirements of a home sale process.

With the arrival of the 1970's, the model changed. The model was affected by the changes in the relocation management companies. While the number of firms calling themselves relocation management firms grew, many of them lacked the capability to provide all the services that were required. They turned to the real estate broker to manage and market the homes they were purchasing. In many cases the relocation management company never saw the property but relied on the eyes and ears of the brokers across the country to tell them about the status of the properties.

Another factor in the rise in the number of relocation departments was that the relocation firms started requesting a centralized process of making referrals to the brokers. Essentially, this meant that for a company with multiple offices, the relocation management company no longer was interested in talking with someone in each and every office to get the home sold. They began requesting that the broker designate a single person to serve as their contact. Many an agent who had worked to develop a clientele of local corporations found that business being pulled away from them as the broker moved to meet the demands of this new client.

This was the era when the brokerage community also began in earnest to deal with the issue of *agency*. One of the long-term dichotomies of the real estate industry was that the brokers found themselves in two worlds at the same time. On one hand, the Internal Revenue Service told the broker that his or her agents were independent contractors. This meant that they could not dictate what hours they worked or tell them what they could or could not do. The individual states, through their real estate laws, said we do not care what the federal government says, you are legally liable for the actions of your agents. Especially in the arena of relocation, the relocation director became the buffer between the two worlds. Remember, most relocation directors were full-time, salaried individuals and had the authority to tell the agents how they would deal with this new business that was coming their way.

The 1970's also saw an increase in the number of referral networks. At one time there were over twenty networks of some kind that were serving the relocation market. These networks mission statements were to be the vehicle for disseminating leads across the country to its members. Each member of the network was given a quota for the number of outgoing referrals they were expected to place within the system. This model did not necessarily push for quality in the referrals, just whether you met your quota on a national basis.

As we ended one decade and entered the next, relocation came into its own as an industry. The various relocation departments became more advanced. A relocation director who was supported by several staff people to handle the referral business replaced the referral coordinator. The department was centralized within the corporate offices and began to develop enhanced packages.

The real estate broker community began to get training specific to relocation. One of the most successful offerings of relocation training came from an organization called *Consultants in Relocation*. Run by Richard Seals, who at one time worked for one of the relocation management companies every year from 1982 to the early 1990's, *Super Session* was designed around a schedule of four workshop sessions per day, containing six different topics per session. The attendees included real estate firm relocation directors and representatives of many corporations and relocation management firms. For those who were new to the industry, it provided the opportunity to learn much of the information discussed in these pages. It allowed them to not only learn their profession but also to network with the very people who could send business their way.

By this time, virtually all the large real estate firms in the country had established separate relocation departments, as had most medium-sized firms. These departments began to expand their services to get into other areas besides home sales to include rental assistance, appraisals, and custom newcomer packets.

The downside to this expansion was that to many relocation management firms, the broker was a necessary evil. I can remember attending a training class in the mid-1980's in which we were clearly told not to discuss the relocation process with the transferee because we did not know what it was that the relocation firms did. The relocation departments were considered to be an island unto themselves. We were there because we could provide a service, and that was the entire picture.

In the 1990's, the real estate firm business model changed again. Many of the relocation departments re-created themselves into mini-relocation management companies. Some even went so far as to begin to buy employees homes using the same system that the bigger firms did. It also was a time that brokers began to look at the cost of delivering services to the industry. The direct result of this review was that many brokers began to unbundle their services. To understand this a little better consider two different scenarios.

In the first scenario, the broker provides to corporations a package of services, which might include, but not be limited to, home finding, home sales, newcomer information, and area tours. These services were provided at no cost to any of the parties in the relocation process. The assumption was that the relocation department could be financed through the volume of the business that was coming to the firm. The brokerage then provided these services at no cost to the industry other than the real estate commissions earned from the sale of homes within their marketplace. However, it became apparent that there were some flaws in this scenario.

The second scenario is the direct result of the review mentioned above. After looking at a true picture of the demands being made on the agents to deliver relocation services, the brokerage began to prepare a list of services available to the industry and charging for each part of the service being delivered. This was also brought about because the referral fees coming from the networks and the relocation management firms began to rise to historical highs.

By the time we reached 2000, the relocation industry had established itself as needed professionals in the process of assisting the transferee get accustomed to the new area. Relocation Directors had also become an integral part of the brokerage management. Relocation Directors were carrying titles such as Vice President or President of the relocation divisions. But the end of the century also saw changes in the business model. These changes will be the subject of the next chapter.

10
PRESENT DAY RELOCATION DEPARTMENT

I n the previous chapter, the development of the relocation departments within the real estate brokerage community was laid out. This chapter will look at the last four years and how the changes in the economic environment are changing the departments once again.

As we entered the twentieth century, the relocation business model changed. It is fully understood that as the business world evolved, the business model would also change.

Before we look at the new business model, it is critical that we understand the previous business model. When the industry began, the model for most of the companies in the field was to charge the corporation a fee, which represented a percentage of the appraised value of the transferee's home. This fee was supplemented by acquiring a small referral fee from the realtor who was assigned to market the property. In the early stages of the industry, this fee amounted to about twenty percent of the referred side of the transaction.

However, the business model changed to the detriment of the very person the relocation industry was supposed to serve. By the year 2000, the delivery of relocation services had moved from being part of the employee benefit to one of being a commodity. The deciding factor on who was selected to provide the relocation services was who had the least impact on the bottom line. As the model changed, the financial picture of the transaction changed. As with any commodity, the client began to look at the proposals purely from the view of who was offering the lowest price. The result was that the margin in each transaction got smaller. The only realistic outcome was to fill the gap with funding from another source. This additional source of revenue became the real estate brokerage referral fees. The relocation departments saw their share of the commission dollars reduced as the level of referral fees escalated from twenty percent to, in some cases, as high as forty percent. Couple this with a rapid increase in the level of home sales across the country, and the relocation director began to encounter agents who made the career decision that handling leads from the relocation department was no longer worth the time or the hassle. They could make more money on business they generated out of their own efforts without referral fees.

Another factor that influenced the relocation departments in the later part of the previous decade and into the current one was the use of after-the-fact referral fees. These occurred when a third-party company would call just prior to a closing and inform the agent that a referral fee

In the old days, the 70's to late 80's, a single referral fee was charged when a relocation company sent a customer to a broker to buy a home. No charge was ever collected when we listed a home by the relocation company. What then became normal was for the Broker to charge his own agents a referral fee of usually five to ten percent on all listings that they got from the relocation department of the broker – who had gotten them with no referral fee from the relocation companies. Then in the late 80's early 90's, some relocation companies, notably Coldwell Banker, started winning contracts by having low or no client feesbut instead went to the brokers and charged twenty-five to thirty percent on all listings. Harvey Auger (former President of Homequity) can distinctly remember going to his broker network advisory board and telling them that if they take business under these conditions, they are forcing all relocation companies to do the same, and it would cost them tremendously. Brokers never refused the business that charged them a referral fee on listings, and as a result, the entire pricing of the industry changed and did not change for the better. Today, some brokers have refused listings because the fees charged are now thirty-five and forty percent, and the agents are refusing the work, but still others are paying it and giving the listings to new agents or agents that are mostly successful because the market will do the work for them. For brokers who are doing it themselves, they are now charging the agents twenty-five to thirty percent and use that as the funding for their departments without having to pay any relocation company. They have reengineered the process and eliminated the

was due based on their contract with the corporation. Failure to agree to the fee could result in the transferee being told that they were not able to complete the transaction.

The result of the two scenarios above resulted in the brokerage community creating their own business model for the present decade. First, many of the brokers recognized that the industry to some degree had lost touch with who the client was. Brokers such as Chip Roach and Wes Foster came to the conclusion that the industry needed to return to servicing the transferee, which was why the industry came into existence in the first place. They achieved this goal by creating divisions within their brokerage operations to function as third-party companies. Many of these brokerage operations are reporting some of the highest revenue figures by returning to the true nature of this industry.

The final look at the industry of today finds many seasoned elders of the industry who claim that the industry today is not any fun anymore. The imposing of greed and cutthroat efforts within the industry has soured many relocation professionals on the future of the industry with many of them considering the possibility of leaving it. I have a close friend who left the industry after almost twenty years and started teaching elementary school age children. Her comment is that working with the children is easier than working within the relocation industry.

Whatever your views of the industry past, present or future, the relocation departments have been a vital part of the relocation industry. The industry has discovered that the real estate brokerage community had a critical role in the delivery of the relocation policy. While some relocation management firms still do this day, look at the real estate agent being part of the process as something to be tolerated, there are still others who recognize the true cooperative contribution that the realtor can make to the process.

The central fact is that without the broker involvement in the process, the process would not have developed the way it has. The broker who truly understands the role of the real estate broker in the process is one who understands the changes relocation has brought to corporate America. Without the trained relocation agent, the level of productivity from the transferee would have been much lower than it has been. The journey through the history of the relocation industry could not be complete without the relocation departments and their services to the transferee.

middle- man. What will really hurt the relocation companies will be when these brokers' relocation arms bring on salespeople that know how to sell to corporate America. Some have, and they are having success, but there still is a long way to go. It should be noted that many of the third-party relocation management staff and the appraisers have also considered leaving the industry due to the purchasing people pressuring the bottom line lower and lower. They have some of the same feelings as the real estate agents who no longer feel the benefit of taking the relocation leads anymore.

Part III

How Do I Get There?

Relocation Policies and the Journey

11
FRAMEWORK FOR RELOCATION

While our journey has covered almost fifty years of development within the relocation industry, there is one aspect of the industry development that I would be remiss in not covering. While we understand the conditions that created the relocation of corporate executives by their employers, there is a piece of the picture missing. As we developed as an industry, there was a requirement brought on by the relocation of corporate executives to develop a system to facilitate the process.

Starting with American Telephone and Telegraph, the corporations set about to develop corporate policies to cover this new benefit for the transferees. The relocation policy became the key to how the transferee got from the old location to the new location. The policy laid out for the employee what the corporation was willing to do for the employee to make the move easier on the family.

The deciding factor as to what was included in the policy was very much dependent on the particular corporate culture of the employer at the time. Looking at the concept of corporate culture, it is possible to identify three types of corporate cultures in the marketplace.

The first form of corporate culture is what we refer to as *womb-to-tomb*. In a corporation centered on this type of culture, the employer did whatever was necessary to make the employee whole after the move. The corporations which held this belief were those who committed to the most inclusive policy. Essentially, whatever the employees needed in the way of support was provided to them. Money was not a factor. This would be especially true of those corporations which moved employees on a regular basis. They needed their employees up and running at full productivity as soon as possible. This could only be achieved by seeing to it that the policy covered every possible circumstance or bump in the road that the employee could be facing. It should be noted here that the corporations which have completed extensive research into their relocation program have discovered that those corporations which value their employees and provide the necessary services to make the moves as easy as possible on the employee and their families gain increased productivity from the employee following the relocation process.

The second form of corporate culture is referred to as *cost-conscious*. Like the womb-to-tomb culture, the employer needs to ensure the productivity of its relocated employees. The difference is that the employer informs the employee that the corporation is more than willing to assist with the problems encountered in relocation but only in consideration of the total budgetary limits of the corporate expenses. The relocation budget is set, and as long as the demands of the employee do not exceed the budget constraints, the corporation is more than willing to assist in the move. It is also this culture group that may very well ask the employee to participate in the costs of the move.

The third form of corporate culture is referred to as *rough justice*. I can give you a perfect example of rough justice. Not too long ago, we made a presentation on utilizing Daniel Bloom and Associates' relocation consulting services. During the presentation I inquired what they did for the candidates they were hiring in the form of relocation policies. The response was that they provided the candidate with a check in the amount of $2,500 and welcomed the candidate to Florida on Monday morning. It made no difference if the candidate needed any other assistance. The flat check was all they got.

The question from each of these culture types is, What message is the employee receiving from the employer. Does the employee believe that the corporation considers them to be a vital part of the corporate community or just some pawn in the completion of some mission decided by the corporate directors?

The remainder of this section is divided into three chapters. Chapter 12 deals with the various components of the policies dealing with the disposition of the current residence. Chapter 13 deals with the policies governing the locating of a new residence and matching the lifestyle the family is used to. Chapter 14 takes a look at those components of the relocation policies which do not necessarily fit into either of the previous categories. This would include such policies as spousal assistance and tax protection.

It should be noted at this juncture that the next several chapters are not meant in anyway to be a treatise on the ins and outs of relocation policy. Instead, it is designed to provide the reader with an overview of the history of policy development. It should also be noted that like everything else in business, the relocation policies have gone through a cyclical process beginning and ending with lump sum allowances.

12
DEPARTURE POLICY COMPONENTS

Pre-Marketing Assistance

It used to be that when an individual had a property to sell, they contacted the local real estate professional, put the home in the multiple listing service for the area, and waited for a buyer to come look at the home. The agent listing the home was either a family friend or the agent who sold them the home when they purchased it.

When working with transferring families, the system becomes a little more complicated. The transferee now has a finite period in which to sell the property and get moved to the new location. The pre-marketing assistance program is designed to achieve three outcomes. First, it discusses how to prepare the property for sale. Second, the transferee is educated on the marketplace. Third, it discusses how to market the home.

Preparing the property for sale

One of the first responsibilities of the relocation-trained real estate professional in the pre-marketing assistance program is to review the property and assist the transferee in preparing the home for the marketplace. This process may mean that carpets need to be changed to be more neutral in color rather than the blatant colors that the transferee thought would not harm his ability to sell the home. The process also looks at the required repairs that any lender will expect before they will write a mortgage against the property.

Education about the marketplace

The second stage involves the real estate professional discussing with the transferee and his or her family the nature of the marketplace. What is the market like today? What are the amenities that most buyers are looking for in their marketplace? What is the trend on prices that are being offered on the properties? Based on these factors, how does the transferee's home fit into the overall marketplace? Based on its current use and condition, what is the maximum dollar value for the property?

How to Market the Home

The relocation management firm also will prepare a report which details for the transferee how it expects to achieve the value that they have determined for the property. This part of the process involves a detailed explanation of the marketing campaign that is planned for the residence. This explanation should include more than just a single statement about the marketing plan for the transferee.

The process is simple in nature. The relocation management company, with the assistance of the local real estate professional, conducts a thorough inspection of the property. Following the inspection, the real estate professional develops a report, which indicates what he found that could detract from the home and, therefore, the price achieved. The report further goes on to explore the value of the repairs and improvements to the transferee's bottom line. The final part of the report is the laying out of the marketing strategy designed to achieve the value stated in the report.

The completed report is sent to the relocation management firm, which reviews the content and conclusions for its completeness. If the report is done correctly, then the relocation management firm advises the real estate professional to set up a second appointment with the transferee to present his or her findings.

Our industry typically requests that two broker reports be completed in order to provide the transferee with some choice. Following the presentation of the report, the transferee can select one of the brokers involved and begin the process of using the report to market the home.

Many corporations use pre-marketing assistance as a way to hold down costs by not having to purchase a home. Pre-marketing assistance further reduces the costs of repairs and improvements to the property because the employee will pay for those repairs as part of the pre-marketing process.

Home Sale Assistance

Home sale assistance refers to those policy components that are implemented after the pre-marketing assistance is completed.

Program Responsibility

One of the first issues to consider when looking at the area of program responsibility is whether you want to offer the program at all. This decision is directly attributable to the corporate culture and transfer volume of your corporation.

In-House Program

What is your corporate culture? Does your corporate philosophy treat your employees as members of the family? If you answered affirmatively to the above questions, the policy may call for you to handle all the moves internally. It is also plausible that if you were dealing with less than fifty moves annually, it would make more sense for you to handle the moves internally. In most in-house purchase programs, the HR function sets up an in-house real estate agency to administer the program. The processes for purchasing the home are in agreement with the industry standards as outlined below.

Third Party Program

Look at your corporate culture once again. If you still want to be of assistance to your employees, but you are short on internal resources, then outsourcing the program to an external expert may be appropriate. Today, there are approximately thirty companies which are in the business of purchasing employees' homes. Each of them uses a standard process for determining the value of the home, which we will discuss later in this chapter.

Financial Responsibilities of the Parties

One final aspect of the question of program responsibility is the question of who bears the financial responsibility at different segments of the program. There are three distinct segments to this process, each having its own specific duties.

The first segment consists of the transferees themselves. They are responsible for all obligations of home ownership until they vacate the property or have accepted the corporate offer on the property, whichever occurs later. Unless other arrangements are made, the title to the property remains in the name of the employee until the close of the sale to the ultimate buyer.

The second segment is the relocation management company, which is responsible for all the costs of the property from the time the transferee vacates the property until the ultimate buyer closes on the property. This means that the relocation management company will make all the payments for the mortgage, taxes, insurance, and maintenance to the property. As part of this process, they will have a deed prepared. This deed will be either a deed-in-blank — in which the transferee signs as the seller and leaves the buyer's name open until one is identified — or as the Employee Relocation Council has suggested, the deed is prepared with the buyer indicated as the corporation or the relocation management firm.

Typically, if they use the two-deed process, the costs of administering the program rise accordingly.

The third segment is that of the client or the corporation. At no time does the corporation become the owner of the property. However, they are responsible for providing working funds to cover all property closing costs, loss on sale, management fees, appraisal fees, and inspection fees.

13

DESTINATION POLICY COMPONENTS

Pre-Purchase Appraisals

Originated by Owens Corning, pre-purchase appraisals were introduced as a means of educating the transferee on the market. It should be stated that they were never designed to save either the transferee or the corporation money. What they were designed to do was to provide the transferee with the knowledge of what a particular property was worth in that place, in that market, and at that time. As the market improved, it no longer became a valuable part of a relocation policy.

Home Finding Assistance

As the industry became more and more sophisticated, the needs of the transferees also became more complex. The goal of the typical employee involved in a relocation process is to duplicate their lifestyle in the new community. The home finding services aspect of the relocation policy was in direct response to the needs of the employees. Home finding assistance included providing the transferee and his or her family with information on schools, recreational activities, cultural life, and guidance as to the types of housing available in the new location. Its purpose was very much in mind when Don McPherson started his counseling service in 1955 with Homerica. The ultimate goal is to as much as possible remove any surprises from the move process. This is in response to the high level of stress caused by a move on all parties involved.

Lump Sum Allowance

As was stated in Chapter Thirteen, the lump sum allowance concept has been around for many years. When the costs of relocation began to escalate, the lump sum concept was applied to the destination end as well as the departure side of the equation. With the arrival of the 1990's, corporations began to tell candidates to whom they had made offers of employment that, upon acceptance of the offer, the corporation would issue to them a check for a certain amount. The caveat in this instance was that the transferee was told that the lump sum allowance was to be used to cover the expenses of the move. However, an added caveat in order to entice the transferee to try and save money on the move was that whatever they did not spend became their signing bonus for coming to work in the new location.

Temporary Housing Assistance

The temporary housing industry began in the 1980's when a company called Oakwood Corporate Housing began to offer corporations an alternative to putting transferees and their families in hotels. This new alternative would provide furnished apartments at a lower cost and provide the transferee with a feeling of being in a home instead of a vacation type of environment. As this new service took off, other companies followed to the point where in the 2004 Worldwide ERC® Roster of Members there are sixty-eight different companies that are offering temporary housing services to corporations across the country.

When the industry moved to a lump sum allowance environment, the use of temporary housing proliferated as the employee tried to save as much of their allowance as possible to use as the signing bonus for joining the corporation.

14

ANCILLARY
SERVICES
POLICY
COMPONENTS

Tax Protection Assistance

During the journey we have undertaken, this policy component has been called by many names. In the early 1980's we called it *gross-up*. For those who have not been in the relocation industry for very long, you have not had the experience of walking into the offices of a human resource director of a corporation and asking them whether they grossed-up. It made for some interesting experiences. Later, the name was changed to *tax liability protection* and then to *tax protection assistance*. Essentially, the policy component provided for the payment of funds to the transferee to help with the tax consequences incurred by moving from the old location to the new location.

Spouse Career Assistance

During the history of the relocation industry, this policy component has been provided under a number of different names. While they all provided essentially the same service, it has been called *spouse assistance, transplacement, family transition services*, and its current name, *spouse/partner career assistance*. In 1986, many transferee's were seen in a private practice setting working with therapists. These mental health professionals were presented with various behavior problems, which could be traced back for a period of eighteen months after a move taking place. The relocations were having a tremendous impact financially on the corporations who were, in some cases, paying for this therapy. Starting with McDonnell Douglas, the industry's pioneer, Laura Herring of the Impact Group became the first company to offer national spouse assistance to transferees and their families. By 1990, there were approximately four firms offering spouse assistance services. Today, there are now at least ten organizations listed in the 2004 Worldwide ERC® Roster of Members and Resource Guide.

There has also been a change in the types of services offered. Today, the spouse/partner assistance program falls into three areas – International Career Continuation, Employee/Family Transition Assistance, and Career Relocation Assistance for Spouse/Partner.

The International Career Continuation assists the spouse/partner who may find themselves in an environment where they are not allowed to work. This service offering works with the spouse to deal with the frustration or anxiety of their situation. An additional part of the service is to help identify alternative activities that can be used to avoid showing a gap in employment while overseas.

Families that take advantage of the employee/family transition service gain a support service for each family member, making life easier and lessening the impact of the stress of a move. It provides the family with a trained individual who can guide them through the everyday acclimation process as they become acclimated to the new area.

The final type of service offered today is the actual career relocation assistance for the other half of the relationship. Its purpose is to accelerate the employment process. It provides the spouse/partner with a go-to person to assist with the employment search.

Payback Agreements

One very perplexing problem for many corporations is how to justify the expenditures for relocating a transferee when there is a real chance that, once the individual has moved to another area on your dime, they then move on to "greener pastures." Starting with such benefit items as tuition, corporations have a policy that if the employee does not stay for a certain period of time, the employee owes the corporation for the amount of reimbursement. Beginning in the 1980's, the use of payback agreements was extended to the relocation arena. Basically, the agreements stated that if the employee accepted a relocation and did not remain with the corporation for a period of at least one year, the employee was required to reimburse the corporation for the relocation expenses that were paid to him or her.

Childcare

Childcare programs have been part of corporate policies since the mid-1940 when Kaiser shipyards opened the first corporate-sponsored child-care centers in Portland, Oregon to reduce the rate of absenteeism among its employees. However, it would not be until the 1970's and 1980's that the real push for these policies would develop. One factor that led to the increase demand was the entrance into the marketplace of the group we commonly refer to as *Generation X*. Many of these workers grew up as *latch key kids*. The name came about from the fact that their parents would send them home from school with a key to the house hung around their necks. They would then be left to their own initiatives on how to pass the time away until the parents came home.

When the members of Generation X entered the workplace, they vowed that they would not treat their offspring in the same manner as they had been treated. Take these conditions and add in the difficulty of finding appropriate, inexpensive options for childcare, the employees began to demand assistance with their childcare needs when they were asked to relocate by their employers.

Today, childcare has become a staple among the various corporate relocation policies that are offered to employees by most of the major corporations and many of the medium-sized firms.

Part IV

The Journey Continues

The Future of the Relocation Industry

15
THE
FUTURE

If you are reading this section of the book, hopefully you did not fast forward to the end thinking you would find the basics of this book. If you have, it is critical that you go back to the beginning of our journey. In order to talk about the future of the industry, it is critical that you have an understanding of where we came from before reaching this point. It has been the intent of this book to provide the reader with a feel for the events and thoughts that led the industry to develop into its current structure.

It is also critical that you realize that relocation, like other business processes, has had the tendency to be cyclical in nature. In 1955, many of the decisions about corporate vendors were the purview of the purchasing departments. As relocation policies began to evolve, these decisions were transferred to the human resource departments. As of late, we have begun to swing back towards purchasing departments making these value decisions. The result has been that over the past decade, the idea of relocation services being delivered to the corporate population has become a true commodity. To drive this point home, there is a Fortune 500 company that named an individual to be the relocation administrator at one of their divisions and gave him the title *Commodity Manager, Relocation*. The problem with relocation being a commodity is that we tend to lose sight of whom we are supposed to be serving as the bottom line. You need to realize that the transferee's perception of the world is, for them, reality. By sending the message that the transferee is nothing more than a commodity, you send the message that as far as the corporation is concerned, the transferee provides nothing of value to its operations.

Neil Rackham and John DeVincentis in their recent book *Rethinking the Sales Force*, make the observation that

Today, customers have many mousetraps to choose from. As far as they are concerned, your mousetrap might have some unique features, but so do 10 competing mousetraps. The customer can substitute one of the alternative competing products for yours and feel perfectly satisfied. What this means is that the bells and whistles you've built into your mousetrap – to mangle the metaphor – no longer add value to the customer. If substitutes are readily available and if the customer sees no extra or unique benefits from your version, then all your marketing and product design efforts are wasted. You may have differentiated your product, but the differentiation doesn't create value because

Taken from *Rethinking the Sales Force* by Neil Rackham and John DeVincentis. Page 10. Printed by McGraw Hill and copyrighted in 1999. Used with permission of John DeVincentis.

it does not matter to the customer. You have become a commodity. As markets commoditize, the amount of value that resides in the product steadily erodes.

Essentially, as we begin to be all the same, our value to the transferee disappears, and the relocation package becomes just another mousetrap like all the rest of the industry.

What is left for our consideration is where this industry will find itself by the time we reach the year 2015 or 2020. Whether a large corporation employs you, a small employer, or even one of the various service firms which represent the end of the chain, you are confronted with some real and critical choices as to the direction your relocation policy is headed. The focus of many corporations has shifted from the *cost of service* to one of the *return on investment* of their human capital. Some corporations will tell you that they dislike putting their personnel in the category with other assets, but the human capital of any organization is as valuable as any of the other asset categories – cost of money, intellectual property, and the real estate that they own. This is plainly discussed in Dr. Jac Fitz-Enz's book *The ROI of Human Capital*.

These critical choices present each and every organization involved with a real dilemma. According to the American Heritage Dictionary of the English Language, 4th Edition, a *dilemma* is a "Situation in which a choice must be made between alternative courses of action or argument." Relocation is an excellent example of being presented with alternative courses of action.

Relocation Dilemma

In every business entity, no matter its size, the human capital population is typically comprised of four very distinctive groups. These groups represent the benefit the corresponding human capital delivers to the corporation and its operations.

The first is what some organizations refer to as *deadwood*. Typically, they are the employees who are barely doing the requisite amount of work to be of any value to the organization. They maintain their positions only because this group is at the bottom of the pyramid. This pyramid represents the contributory value of the position to the overall operation of the entity. The higher you go in the pyramid the more valuable you as an employee are to the daily operations.

Dr. Fitz-Enz is the founder of the Saratoga Institute and one of the foremost experts in the human resources profession today. His book looks at how a corporation can measure the economic value of employee performance within their operations.

The second group is represented by the individuals who are valuable employees and who would move if you asked them to, only if they could. Unlike the deadwood, they are truly valuable employees and demonstrate their value to the mission statement of the corporation each and every day. Due to family considerations or other commitments, though, they are just unable to accept a relocation assignment if it became available. In this case, relocation would be real hardship on both the employee and the family unit.

The third group is represented by those valuable employees who will go anywhere and do anything that their employer asks them to do. They are the individuals who at one time thought nothing of being asked to relocate every two years – and doing so. These are also the employees that the corporation considers to be in a critical position for the success of the corporation. They are the one group who needs and expects a complete package of relocation benefits if they were accepting a change in assignment. They are looking for the corporation that realizes that relocation brings about some very dramatic changes in the lifestyles of the family, and there are times when extra support is a necessity.

The employee who may be at the end of his career represents the last of our groups, and the acceptance of a relocation may not make sense to the employee or the family members. They feel that it is in their best interests to remain in their current location for the remaining years of their work lifetime. As will be demonstrated later in this chapter, there may be a way to utilize their talents in a relocation environment and have the situation be good for both sides of the equation.

Sooner or later, every organization will suffer the loss of a critical employee to the operation. How the vacancy is handled is clearly dictated by the internal corporate culture of the organization as we discussed in Chapter 11. We can further demonstrate the impact of these cultural types by looking at the diagram on the next page.

The Relocation Dilemma

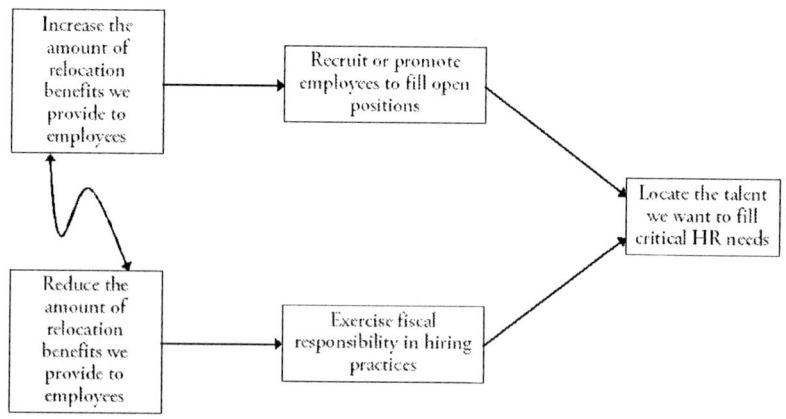

Eliyahu Goldratt followed *The Goal* with *It's Not Luck* in 1994, *Critical Chain* in 1997 and *Necessary But Not Sufficient* in 2000. Each takes the concepts that were developed in the first book and carries them through other aspects of the business operation. For further information on these titles and the *Theory of Constraints* visit the Goldratt Institutes website located at goldratt.com.

Prior to discussing the implications of the diagram above, it is beneficial to stop and take a minute to review how the diagram was constructed. In 1984, an Israeli physicist named Eliyahu M. Goldratt, wrote a business-oriented novel called *The Goal*. This book is used by many of the MBA programs in the country as a required text. In the book and a subsequent three books, Goldratt laid out what he refers to as the *Theory of Constraints*. The Theory of Constraints in essence states that during any process, there are always processes which are holding up the rest of the flow throughout the remainder of the system. With the help of Dr. James Holt of the University of Washington in Vancouver, I took the basis of the Theory of Constraints and applied it to relocation for the first time in an article entitled "Driving the Relocation 500" which appeared in the October 2001 issue of *Mobility Magazine*. In the relocation arena, that constraint is the process of getting the employee moved and returned to productivity. To further demonstrate how the process is implemented, I suggest to the reader that they assume that the decision to relocate an employee has already been made.

The reasoning behind the dilemma is that any opening within the corporate structure has a direct impact on both the morale and the productivity of the organization. As corporate America discovered during the period of re-engineering or rightsizing, every position within an organization is given the responsibility for a prescribed set of duties and functions. When a position sits vacant, the workload does not just disappear; it must be completed in some fashion. The "simplest" method to solve the problem is to pass the extra workload on to the other members of the department to keep the ship afloat. Just because a position is vacant does not mean that the organization ceases to perform these duties.

The result is that some projects will be completed on time, while other projects will not be completed because there is just not enough time in the day to finish everything. This leads to lower morale and, more importantly, lower productivity.

Returning to the previous diagram, you can see that the dilemma paradigm begins with the decision as to whether or not the position should be filled.

Corporation Must Locate the Talent to Fill Critical HR Needs

An integral part of your corporate structure, the human resources organization is faced with several charges.

The first is that human resources, in conjunction with management, must make the decision as to whether or not the corporation will even fill the vacant positions and, if so, how. When an opening does appear, the corporation is faced with several options. The most apparent option is that it can recruit someone to fill the position. However, it can also choose not to fill the position at all. Instead, human resources could turn to an outside firm, such as a Personnel Employment Organization or HR organization, to assume the duties of the departing employee through the use of contract personnel.

The second charge after you have made the decision to hire or promote someone into the position is to do so in the most cost-effective manner possible. We are talking here about one of the four assets at the disposal of any organization, human capital. Are we concerned with the cost of money, which will affect the immediate bottom line, or are we concerned with the human capital asset of the organization? When we begin to look at the process of locating the right talent to fill our needs from a cost of money aspect, as the relocation industry is doing today, the package of relocation services has no value to the transferee – and we have just relegated the employee's importance to the level of a commodity. As Rackham and DeVincentis stated in the excerpt from *Rethinking the Sales Force*, the more a product or service becomes a commodity, the less value the customer realizes. When the primary decision maker in the selection of a vendor to handle relocation becomes the purchasing department, we erode the value of those services. The flip-side of the coin appears to be that, if instead of the cost-of-money we view the process from a human capital asset perspective, then the question is whether there is money to be saved by covering the costs of the relocation more fully at the outset of the relocation.

When looking deeper into this question, we find that in order to recruit or promote employees to fill the critical human capital needs, several reasons require the corporation to increase the amount of relocation benefits they provide.

The first reason is that the corporation must meet the needs of the relocating families. Many within the relocation industry recognize that the process of undergoing a relocation is very stressful on every aspect of the family. The relocation process is stressful not only for the immediate family but the extended family as well. The demands of settling in a new location are different for each family that enters the process. In order to achieve a successful relocation, the corporation must be willing to develop a unique package of services which meets the very specific needs of the transferees and their immediate families.

The second reason for increasing relocation benefits is that in order to recruit or promote employees to fill the available human resource needs, the corporation must remain competitive in the marketplace. The difficulty with the availability of human capital within the workplace is that it is finite. There are just so many individuals available for each open position. Whether the corporation is a member of the Fortune 1000 or a small emerging firm, each corporation is seeking to replace the departing employee with an equally or more talented one from the same pool of qualified candidates. Therefore, whether the corporation wants to admit it or not, they are in a bidding war for the available talent. It is not uncommon for individuals, especially if they are members of what we refer to as Generation X, to be looking for very specific things in their lives. They can take the time to do "Ben Franklin Closes" on the various relocation options that are presented to them. It therefore becomes paramount that the corporation establishes relocation benefits which are, at a minimum, on par with the other corporations in their industry that the same human capital assets are considering.

The third reason is that relocation benefits are a cost of doing business in the marketplace. The goal in locating or promoting an individual to fill a critical opening is to fill the gap in the workflow. During the period of vacancy, workloads had to be spread over other individuals who had other regular duties and now have to take over these projects also. The cost of providing relocation services is worth the cost to return the work distribution to its normal levels.

Another reason for recruiting new talent to the organization is that to remain competitive, the corporation must continually refresh the outlook of the talent base. We live in a rapidly changing world. Industry is making new discoveries that can change the configuration of our lives on a daily basis. If your organization is staffed with nothing but long timers, the thought processes can become stale in nature. The new talent, especially representatives of different generations such as Generation X or Y, brings new insight from the world to the organization.

If we return to the lower part of the diagram, we find the focus changes to the other two types of corporate culture — cost-conscious or rough justice. In the upper part of the diagram, we were looking at a corporate culture that represented the womb-to-tomb environment. Here we are looking at an environment where the corporation is trying to recruit the required new talent but restricts the amount of spending that is designated for relocation policies. The reasons behind this altered perspective are several.

The first reason is that the management of the organization feels that its first duty to the organization is to maintain a proper level of funding for the operations of the corporation. The assumption is that the total amount of funds available is set at a particular number. This number means that there is just so much funding available for each segment of the operation. In many business environments, the human resources department receives the short end of the stick.

The second reason why the bottom of the diagram exists is the feeling that supposedly, for the morale of the corporation, the benefit packages must be equitable to all the employees within the organization. No one should be provided with any more benefits than the next employee in line. It doesn't matter whether the individual involved is filling a critical human capital need or not.

The third reason for the bottom of the diagram is that to keep costs in line, the corporation must eliminate any and all extraneous perks. This can be seen not only in the relocation arena but also across the board in the human resources arena. This can be seen in the trend to lessen retirement benefits and to make the employee cover more of their health care costs.

The view as to what constitutes extraneous benefits is rooted in the beliefs of the upper management of the corporation. I recently had a client who was trying to recruit some critical human capital assets, and one of the applicants requested assistance with the sale of his current residence. The Chief Executive Officer's response was, He did not receive any assistance in this area, so why should we help lower-level employees?

If we look at the first two blocks of the diagram, we are presented with a very real conflict that is the root of the dilemma. On the one hand, we need to increase the amount of relocation benefits we provide in order to recruit the very real required human capital assets needed to move the corporation forward in the marketplace. On the other hand, we need to reduce the relocation benefits we provide all the employees within the organization.

The dilemma is that we can't have both because relocation benefits first of all cost money. Even more importantly, these benefits are a necessity in the competition for human capital to use as a recruiting tool. The final reason why we cannot have both is that we cannot change the focus of the recruiting effort and still remain competitive. We fully realize that relocation is becoming more and more expensive. Since 1955 the cost of moving an employee and his family has risen continually. I fully recognize that corporations need to be fiscally responsible with how they spend the corporate funds. However, the question is, Are they spending those monies in a way that will perpetuate the competitive standing of the corporation in the marketplace?

Every year the Worldwide ERC® has conducted a survey in order to determine the costs being paid by corporations to relocate an employee to a new location. See chapter endnote 1 for the data from those surveys.

Having considered the relocation dilemma, what are the trends that will have a direct effect on the future of the relocation industry? When I look at the future of the relocation industry, there appear to be eleven primary trends that will make or break the industry in the years to come:

Trend One: Lack of New Talent in the Industry
Trend Two: Lack of Integrity within the Industry
Trend Three: Presence of Human Resource Organizations
Trend Four: Looming Talent Shortage
Trend Five: The Distribution of Work
Trend Six: New Employee Focus
Trend Seven: Better Retention of the Human Capital Assets
Trend Eight: Minimized Role of Relocation in the Corporate World

Trend Nine: Loss of the industry Vision
Trend Ten: Need for Value-Added Delivery
Trend Eleven: Better Understanding of the Real Costs of Relocation

In the pages that follow, I will look at these trends and how they will shape the future of the relocation industry.

Trend #1: Lack of new talent coming into the industry

In the introduction to this journey that we are now completing, I mentioned that the impetus for this book was an article that I wrote for *Mobility Magazine* in 1992. The article entitled "Where have all the elders gone?" was a look at the dilemma faced by this industry. Individuals who are assigned to the relocation function share two very distinct traits. The first is that typically they have been in the assignment less than five years. The modern day relocation administrator has no clue as to how we got to the situation we are discussing today. Even more tragic for the industry's future is the fact that relocation has become a place where you hang your hat for a short respite on your climb up the corporate ladder. It is not a point where someone is likely to make a career for the rest of his or her employment years.

In many cultures, the elders of the industry are given the responsibility of passing on the knowledge of the previous generations to new blood. That has not happened within the relocation industry. As the years pass by, the elders are making the choice to leave the industry. Some of this migration is due to retirement. Still others have become tired of the industry and have made the choice to go to other pastures. The Real Estate Community no longer has Super Session. The Certified Relocation Professional™ and the Global Mobility Specialist™ sponsored by the Worldwide ERC® are great programs to provide the participant with information about modern day trends within the industry. However, by no means does either of these programs go in-depth into the history of the industry. In many cases, after almost half-a-century, people are still entering this industry by a "fluke of nature." There is nobody that I am aware of that has made the conscious decision as they leave high school to make the commitment to become a relocation specialist. But if the industry is to continue, we need as an industry to provide an avenue to encourage individuals to do just that.

To accomplish this goal, the industry needs to begin to push for the creation of courses at the college level to acquaint and train prospective new relocation professionals with a solid foundation in the industry. These courses could be part of the core requirements for a degree in corporate relocation or as a track within the human resource curriculum. Another option could be to create a certificate program in relocation similar to the Society of Human Resource Management Association's Professional Human Resource (PHR) Certification program.

This foundation should present a total picture of the relocation industry – past, present and future. It should involve the participant in a course of interdisciplinary studies designed not only to look at what the industry is doing but also why we are doing it. It needs to take into account every facet of the business organization that directly or indirectly has an influence on the relocation process. To achieve this required knowledge base, the individual needs to be exposed, I believe, to a logical progression of ideas. To achieve this I would suggest that the proposed curriculum offer the prospective relocation professional the following course configuration.

The sequence of topics used in this section are based on the material used in Robert L. Mathis' Human *Resource Management 7ᵗʰ Edition* which is used by many of the courses for the PHR certification by the Society for Human Resource Management.

Course 1: Introduction to Relocation

This introductory course would provide the student with an overview of the relocation process and the part it plays in the development of human capital assets. It would also begin a consideration of the idea of a supply chain for services and how the parts are integrated in the delivery function.

Course 2: Relocation History and Demographics

In the presentation of Part 1 of this book, we discussed to some degree how the demographics of the workplace have changed and how these changes brought about an increase in corporate relocations. This course would cover the same information in far more detail. The emphasis would be in correlating the cultural history along with the changes in the business community. It would explore how the major events in history actually changed the way we did things from a business point-of-view.

The other part of this second course would be a look at the changing demographics. Over the course of the journey, we have seen three generations enter the marketplace and are poised on the introduction of a fourth. It is critical that the new relocation professional understands what each of these generations demanded from their quality of life and workplace environment.

Course 3: Basics of Relocation Finance

The purpose of this third course would be the implication of the financial aspects of the relocation business. This would include a look at the accounting principles involved in the calculations of relocation costs, the tax implications of the various relocation policy components, and the effect on the employee.

Another aspect of this part of the curriculum would be an in-depth look at the process used by a purchasing department in making the buy decision for purchasing relocation services. This should especially include a look at the Request for Proposal (RFP) process and how the intent of the process is related to the financial responsibilities of the corporation. This means that the student needs to gain a true understanding of the cost of money. It would also take the concepts developed in the first course about the supply chain and present them in real time regarding the supply chain in the relocation function. They need to understand how procurement works as a rule in corporate America.

Course 4: The Human Resources Function

Of all the various assets that a corporation has, the human capital asset is the most critical to the whole concept of relocation. Robert Martin's text, in fact, would make a good basis for this particular course. The sequence of topics walks the student through the process of human resource management. During the duration of this course, the student is presented with a number of distinct areas of concentration.

The first area of concentration looks at the perspectives of human resource management. The student learns about the transitional nature of the human resource function. Over the years, HR has been called many names, but the important issue is how the function has evolved over the decades that our journey has covered. As the names have changed, so has the role of HR within the corporate hierarchy. This role has changed from being a necessary evil to one of a strategic partner within the corporation and the external marketplace. The student needs to understand these changing roles. The student also gets their first look at the various costs involved in the HR management arena and how they affect the activities of the department relocation, related or not.

With the scandals at Enron, Worldcom/MCI, and the passage of the Sarbanes-Oxley Act, the student needs to consider the various ethical issues involved with the HR activity spectrum and with relocation in particular.

Another aspect of the curriculum is to convince the prospective new relocation professional that relocation is a worthwhile career choice. It is therefore critical that we discuss with the student the benefits of a career in human resources. The only way to present this concept is to have the student interface with individuals who are already making HR and relocation a career.

As we entered the new century in 2000, we became faced with an increasingly growing global workplace and workforce. Part of the curriculum then needs to look at the role of diversity and global issues within the workforce. How do we treat the fast-track employee who is moved overseas when he returns? What do we do to reap the benefits of new experiences on the future of the corporate hierarchy?

Nothing in the workplace happens by total surprise. Many of the changes that take place in the human resources arena are the direct result of strategic planning. There is no corporation that I know of that makes decisions about moving an employee by throwing a dart at the wall and, wherever it lands is who is being relocated tomorrow. The decision about who is going is made depending on the department's strategic planning and the reporting department's manpower needs. Where and when are the human capital assets needed the most? How are the changing demographics characterized? Identifying the characteristics of the current workforce, can we find the talent we need when we need it? How does the supply and demand of talent affect workforce adjustments?

The fourth area of HR management responsibilities is that of equal employment. Whether we are talking about equal employment based on the law of the land, or we are talking about the diversity of the workforce, the corporation needs to ensure that each individual who is qualified and eligible is given the opportunity to apply for relocation to another position if it makes sense for both the employee and the employer. This is true if for no other reason than further protecting the assets of the corporation from danger.

We have already discussed superficially the question of the human capital assets of the marketplace. We have talked about the dilemma that relocation confronts for most corporations. This next area prepares the relocation professional to understand the role of recruiting within the human resource function. How are we going to locate the talent we need? Even more important for the corporation, once we recruit the talent we need, how are we going to retain that talent for future years?

The final area of this part of the program would be a review of compensation packages for employees, both current and newly hired. This would include an in-depth look at relocation policy components. In the previous part of the book, we looked at the policies from the point of view of their evolution. This part of the curriculum would look at each of the relocation policy components not only from this perspective but also from the point of view of how they are implemented within the policy packages.

Course 5: Basics of Relocation Law

While I do not expect any of the participants of this curriculum to become practicing attorneys and members of the Bar, it is, however, important that they understand the legal aspects of the relocation process.

Every aspect of the process inevitably has a legal impact on the transferee and the corporation. As a result, whether we are talking about moving expenses, home-sale assistance, or the providing of relocation loans, the relocation professional needs to have a working knowledge of what is happening to the transferee. I am not suggesting that he or she will become a walking expert, but they need to be able to make a reasonable judgment about the legal ramifications of the relocation package on the employee's tax liability.

Course 6: Basics of Relocation and Real Estate

The next area that the curriculum would need to investigate is the impact of the real estate laws on the relocation process. This impact not only covers the home sale and home purchase aspects of the real estate transaction but also the question of disclosure of environmental issues and material defects in the property.

One alternative for presenting the subject matter might be to have the course material mirror the state's real estate licensing law. Having the professional actually complete and earn a state real estate license should be considered.

Trend #2: Lack of integrity within the relocation industry

With almost every delivery of the daily newspaper or broadcast of the nightly news, we are confronted with stories about the ethics of our business leaders. The relocation industry has not been immune to this trend.

During the course of our journey, the relocation industry has undergone some very dramatic changes. None has been greater than the loss of integrity among some participants in the industry. Note that I said *some*, not *all*, of the participants within the industry.

So what kind of situations am I referring to? I am referring to actions by certain members of this industry who act in a manner that is contrary to the best interests of the end user in the relocation process-the transferee.

The relocation industry is one of those industries in the marketplace where there is no financial trail as to where the funds are spent. The relocation companies have routinely charged their clients a percentage of the appraised value as a service fee. Some have lately tried charging either a flat fee or no fee at all. Corporations have begun to question the escalating costs of relocation and the impact of these costs on the human capital asset return on investment. But *at no time* has the majority of the industry laid out in plain graphic style the flow of money and the cost of money in delivering the service package.

Another aspect of this integrity question is that there have been companies who found that some of their vendors were also calling on other corporations for their business. In retaliation, they told the vendor that they were being removed from the list of preferred vendors. The end result is that the vendor is given the choice of losing one source of business to try and replace it with one that they have created.

In other cases, companies began to ask for referral fees that they were not entitled to but demanded anyway. They did so under the premise that it was "play the game or lose the closing income." The question of after-the-fact referral fees has become an issue. Understand that I fully recognize the right of a service provider to make a dollar, but I do not recognize their right to try and earn the dollars by back door efforts.

The relocation industry was created in the early 1950's to assist the transferee with one of the most difficult decisions they would make in a lifetime. The trend to turn the process of helping a transferee into a pure number decision does not do justice to the reason why this industry began. We are forgetting who is the one who gets hurt the most here. By equating relocation benefits to dollars-and-cents, we are telling our human capital that they are really nothing more than a number.

If the industry is to survive the next fifteen years, then making the true cost of delivering relocation services transparent is not only good policy but it is also the right thing to do. The only reason why a service provider would not do so is if it has something to hide. In order to maintain the level of service the transferee is receiving, all the vendors must disclose the track of funds from receipt to the bottom line. When I say all the vendors, I mean the relocation firms, the real estate agent, the title company, the household goods companies, and the mortgage firms among the many assisting with the industry efforts to assist the transferee.

Trend #3: Presence of Human Resource Organizations

Almost every day we can open the newspaper and read about another company that has outsourced one or more of their human resource functions. One organization that is picking up on this trend is the Human Resource Organization or the Personnel Employer Organization (PEO).

Essentially they come into a company and offer to assume the obligations for compensation, benefits, insurance etc, freeing up the corporate staff to concentrate on building the business. The direct result of this trend is that more and more corporations are taking a real hard look at what these organizations have to offer.

The PEO market represents one of the largest groups of human resource consultants in the country from a revenue perspective. They offer a program under which the PEO supplies the staff to the corporation and assumes the costs of the employee working for them. While this is not the place for a detailed explanation of the workings of these organizations, we do need to state that they open the strong possibilities that the relocation industry will have a new type of client on the market. They provide a cost-cutting service to their clients by being able to reduce benefit costs by purchasing the services in bulk.

The question we would pose to the reader is, If the Human Resource Organization is growing in scope, and it is controlling a majority of the workforce, who is going to help it relocate its staff as the need permits? Truly, the Personnel Employer Organizations will be the next new client for the relocation industry. This applies if you are the relocation management firm or the real estate broker.

Trend #4: Coming labor shortage

There is much discussion in the human resource arena today as to whether or not we are headed into another labor shortage.

In a recent issue of *HR Magazine*, Robert J. Grossman stated that,

Robert J. Grossman is a lawyer and a professor of management studies at Marist College. His article in the March 2005 issue of *HR Magazine* was entitled "The Truth About the Coming Labor Shortage."

based on information that he received from the Bureau of Labor Statistics, the predictions are off-base. His contention is that the data is flawed when you look at the level of total jobs in the future and the number of workers available to fill those positions. This is due to the fact that the data used to calculate the figures are derived from two sets of numbers, which are not compatible. However, Grossman does recognize that the labor shortage is true, and that the upper end of the high-technology job applicants will become less and less as the years get closer to 2017.

In 2001, Watson Wyatt, a nationally known HR consulting firm, released a report that indicated that, at the time of the report, there were just over one million open jobs in the information technology field. Based on the demographics of the workforce, they envisioned no end in sight for the demand for these workers. By the time we reach the year 2017, at the present rate there will be more IT professionals retiring from the workforce then are making the decision to enter the field.

In still more evidence of the pending labor shortage, we need only turn to the work of Charles Grantham and James Ware at the Work Design Collaborative. The Collaborative has conducted or been involved in research which indicates that what Richard Florida referred to as the *Creative Class* will make up the labor gap that is coming by 2007. In some cases this gap is here now. The problem is that when the economic growth level remains under 2.5%, many companies can, in essence, sweep the problem under the carpet. The reality is that as economic growth increases, the professionals who make up the creative class are going to be placed in an all out bidding war. As we will discuss in more detail below, the high-knowledge employee will be able to set the criteria for the amount of relocation benefits that are delivered to encourage them to move.

In order for the relocation industry to survive to the year 2020, corporate America is going to have to wake up to the fact that they are creating problems for themselves by changing the nature of how relocation benefits are delivered to the employees they are trying to recruit.

Trend #5: Distribution of work

In conjunction with the aforementioned trend regarding the coming labor shortage, those candidates are going to be looking at their opportunities with a different vision. There is no longer a stringent requirement in their eyes that they have to move to Ann Arbor, San Francisco, or New York. The candidate is going to be in the driver's seat and will tell the

Further information about the work force collaborative can be found on the web at futureofwork.com

Richard Florida, a cartographer with Carnegie Mellon University, has described the marketplace being divided into four primary groups. The first group, or the Creative Class, includes such professions as the healthcare professionals, corporate managers, lawyers, business occupations, teachers, information technology specialists, and the arts and design professionals. The second group is the working class that covers the repair services, corporation not only how they are going to work but also where.

With the introduction of increasingly sophisticated technology, any given employee can work from anywhere they want and still perform the duties required by the employer. Video conferencing allows the employee to sit in his home and still attend meetings. On-line learning platforms allow for projects to be conducted in real-time.

For corporations and relocation management firms looking to survive to the year 2020, learning to live with flexible, customized relocation packages is vital. The day of one-size-fits-all packages is gone. Each relocation assignment will need to be specifically designed for the wants and needs of the transferee. The corporation can no longer tell the employee of the next decade that they absolutely have to move to any one particular location. If you believe it won't work, take a close look at the military. They have been creating customized relocation programs for their personnel for a number of years.

construction services, production occupations, and the transportation occupations. The third group is the service class, which contains the many hourly jobs that are found in the marketplace. The final class is comprised of the agricultural worker class.

Trend #6: New employee focus

The new employee is not the employee of the early days of the industry. Then, the traditionalist and early baby boomers went where they were told to go. They firmly believed that their corporate careers depended on their accepting any relocation offer which was presented to them. Today's employee – and employees of the years to come – will begin to put more emphasis on both the quality of life and the cost of living in the area where the new employment is located. Let's look at these issues in a little more detail.

The new employee's focus is, first of all, How much is it going to cost me to live there? Are you asking them to move to places like the Northeast where by the time you pay your federal, state, and local tax burdens you are left with a small amount left to pay for the necessities of life – much less any expenditures such as cultural, recreational, or other pursuits. You purchase a home, and the majority of your discretionary income goes to paying for it. I can remember getting a phone call from my mother telling me that the son of one of the families who lived on the street where I grew up had just bought their first home for $999,000. The new employee will ask, "Is it worth it?"

The second and more critical element is the nature of the quality of life that the new employee is looking for in the new location. They are not willing to settle for just any quality of life. They want very specific answers to that question.

Richard Florida indicated in his book that the creative class members are seeking an area with authentically-built architecture, authentic restaurants (meaning not chains), and a diversity of lifestyles. The new employee is looking for a work environment where the work/life situation is in balance. The Generation X members of the workforce are willing to stop work on a project so that they can attend the son or daughter's soccer game or school play. Family life is as important as the life at work.

The impact for the future of the industry is that corporate higher management needs to begin to rethink its view of relocation. Where can we move an individual that will fulfill the needs of the corporation and the employee at the same time? They will have to arrange their employee movements around the wants of the transferee. It will be imperative that both human resources and purchasing operate in sync with each other, not utilizing just their own agendas. While costs are still a factor, the long-term contribution of the employee is critical to the bottom line of the corporation. The two units must look at what is feasible for the corporation in order to ensure that they can control the talent gap.

Trend #7: Better Retention of human capital assets

Every corporation, no matter its size, has to maintain and nurture four types of assets that are common to every operation. The first asset is the *real estate* that they own. Where are their operations housed? The second asset is the *cost of money*. What does it cost to maintain the programs, products and services of the corporation? The third asset is the *technology* that corporation owns. These technologies represent the various advancements that the corporation has made to the civilization in which we live.

The final and possibly the most critical asset to the success of the operation is its *human capital* assets. They represent the creative mind of the corporation. Every new product or service that the corporation offers is the direct result of the interaction of the creative minds of its employees. During our journey, corporate America found what it thought was the answer to all answers in a process, introduced by Michael Hammer, called *re-engineering.*

Re-engineering, in itself, was a great idea. It suggested that by reviewing the total corporate structure, we could remove parts of the organization that would increase the effective parts of the operation. The problem was that as the employee level decreased, the workload increased.

Another aspect of the re-engineering process was that we found that the so-called brain knowledge was among the casualties. What corporations discovered post-re-engineering was that the very human capital assets that were needed in the future for the extra workload were the very assets that re-engineering kicked unceremoniously out the door.

In order for the corporation and the relocation industry to survive into the next decade, the corporation must realize that it is paramount for them to stop the brain knowledge loss. This means that we need to look again at the reasons why we are starting relocation in the first place.

Part of this effort to better retain the talent we need to survive as a corporation may very well mean that we need to rephrase the questions we are asking to our employees. Instead of asking them about schools, real estate, and moving needs, direct the questions instead to the idea of what do they want to do with the rest of their lives. Instead of having an employee who is close to retirement turn down a relocation, the industry must ask them where might they want to retire to. Using the capabilities of the new technologies, can we move them there now and let the employee work from home? Can we facilitate the acquisition of the desired life styles they are seeking? We as relocation professionals are left with only one option – do it or lose the very talent we need to survive the next several decades.

Trend #8: Minimized role of relocation within the corporate world

Relocation has become a commodity. There is no disputing this fact. The Fortune 100 corporation which named its relocation manager Commodity Manager, Relocation tells us that. With the ever increasing costs of relocation, we realize that the reasoning behind the purchasing involvement in the relocation process makes sense.

Make no mistake about it: the problem is that despite the image or message that this policy sends to the marketplace, the transferee does not consider himself to be a commodity. It must be emphasized that *perception is reality* to the transferee. So if his perception says that he does not believe that he is a commodity, then the minimizing of the role in relocation will hurt the corporation in the long run.

To survive to 2020, the corporate world must return to a culture where the worth of the human capital assets are publicly recognized. We must augment the services we obtain from the human resource organizations to include counseling in the areas of financial planning, specific area counseling, and alumni clubs which can serve as mentors to the new employee relocating to an area. With this in mind, we must discover workable ways to extend the tenure of employees who may not be ready to leave the corporate world at sixty-two or sixty-seven. We need to extend to these employees who are staying on longer a way to stay connected to both the corporate world and quality of life issues that they are seeking.

Trend #9: Loss of the vision of why the industry started

As we reach the end of the first four years of the new millennium, our industry has lost sight of why we were created in the first place. We have forgotten who the true end-user is of our services. This industry was formed to facilitate the movement of transferees of the corporation, in order to provide them with the basis for a new life and the return to productivity in as little time as possible.

With the change of perspective to a commodity, the focus moved from the employee to the bottom line of the corporation. There is no in-between. The transferee no longer sees any benefit to the relocation process. They are no longer willing to blindly accept the move.

It is therefore critical at this juncture that we return to the vision of 1955. The reason for this industry in the first place was to meet the needs of the corporate transferee. The needs may have changed, but the final focus for relocation professionals cannot. We must reinvent our service package to bring back that early vision which provided the basis for the industry. There are ways that we can assist the transferee and still help the corporate bottom line as we will discuss in Trend #11.

Trend #10: Value added delivery

In the beginning, the sales point for what the industry did was the added value to the transferees by assisting them with the trauma of relocating. When we became a commodity, there no longer was any value delivered to the transferee; they became a number not an asset.

To return to a value-added delivery model, we must determine what the anticipated outcome of the move is. Are we looking for an up and coming employee who is just starting his career? Or are we assisting the employee with the pre-retirement period of his career, and so we can assist him in getting to his planned final location ahead of the retirement time?

We need to review the value of the relocation process to all parties to of the transaction. If we are not providing value, we need to change how we deliver the product so that value is present.

Relocating an employee for the sake of moving them without an exit strategy is a waste of resources of both the corporation and the employee. We must recognize that the value proposition is going to be different to each and every customer, and we must be ready and capable to be flexible in how we deliver our product to meet these different views. We must investigate up front what are the particular requirements of this employee in order to maintain this employee as a valuable contributing member of the corporate community.

Trend #11: Better understanding of the true cost of relocation benefits

The final trend that will determine the future of the industry is that we must gain a true understanding of the true cost of the provision of relocation benefits. Remember, we have said that relocation benefits are a cost of doing business. These costs can be looked at from either a short- or long-term view.

The short-term view says that we are in a cost conscious or rough justice type of culture. We constantly see the bottom line as the guiding light as to what we can provide to an employee. The very decision whether to move an employee is based on what will the financial impact be on the corporation to make the move. The concern is not the well being of the transferee but rather what the impact will be on the corporation. The short-term view does not take into consideration the costs of a failed relocation, because that becomes another issue.

On the flip side of the coin is the long-term view. In this scenario we recognize the true costs of the relocation. We know that in any given situation we have the employee's salary and benefits. They represent the annual salary with an additional thirty-five percent, or more, added cost for benefits. The corporation expects a certain level of service from the employee in return for relocating them to the new location.

If the relocation should fail, the corporation is then confronted with the initial costs plus the re-spending of the costs to recruit a replacement. These costs include the moving costs and the retraining time. It includes the downtime, productivity-wise, as they get moved. It includes the costs of getting the family settled in the new area for a second time,

As relocation professionals the duration of this industry lies in your hands. You decide whether we meet the needs and perceptions of the transferees. You decide whether we live in a world of care for the welfare of the employee base of the organization or whether we consider them to be just another pawn in the business world. Do we think of the employee as more or less an inanimate object who is there to fulfill a cog in the business machine? Do we look at relocation benefits as something we did once and would prefer not to ever have to deliver again?

By following us through this journey, you now know that the transferee's bottom-line perspective is to match their quality of life. Having said that they are primarily concerned with the idea of "Just get me there." They do not care how you do it, just do it.

By truly understanding these eleven trends, we can get them there with a lower level of stress and a higher level of productivity. We just need to remember the value vision of this industry when it began and bring it back to the process.

End Notes

Note 1 – The costs being paid by corporations to relocate an employee to a new location.

Year	Current Employee Owner	Current Employee Renter
1978	$12,787	$ 4,217
1979	$15,808	$ 4,952
1980	$20,886	$ 5,964
1981	$26,432	$ 7,366
1982	$31,100	$ 8,100
1983	$31,961	$ 8,917
1984	$32,846	$ 8,663
1985	$32,303	$ 9,124
1986	$33,381	$ 9,164
1987	$35,705	$10,115
1988	$37,127	$10,880
1989	$39,660	$10,649
1990	$42,585	$11,234
1991	$46,667	$12,290
1992	$45,330	$12,457
1993	$45,263	$11,960
1994	$44,920	$12,366
1995	$45,373	$12,962
1996	$47,776	$13,642
1997	$51,930	$14,210
1998	$53,696	$15,604
1999	$51,353	$15,335
2000	$57,279	$16,701
2001	$60,931	$18,564
2002	$65,555	$18,944

Year	New Hire Owner	New Hire Renter
1985	$21,700	$5,773
1986	$22,737	$6,074
1987	$23,501	$6,627
1988	$25,906	$6,910
1989	$26,587	$6,648
1990	$29,734	$7,530
1991	$33,467	$8,227
1992	$32,255	$8,346
1993	$34,600	$8,486
1994	$35,902	$8,948
1995	$35,382	$9,280
1996	$37,457	$9,767
1997	$37,835	$10,390
1998	$40,676	$11,491
1999	$41,780	$11,072
2000	$45,948	$13.456
2001	$49,469	$14,001
2002	$55,212	$15,079

16
AFTERWORD

Back in the early days of this industry, there was a fairly popular television show that had as its theme an encounter with a particularly noted individual on each show. The emcee would introduce the star and then reach behind a chair and produce a large book. The show continued with the emcee stating "Mr. Star, This is Your Life!" Over the next half hour to an hour, various individuals came on stage to discuss events in the life of the individual.

In that light, this journey has been relocation's version of *This is Your Life*. It has been a journey that has been seen from the eyes of those who were there to live it as it happened. For the "youngsters" who are reading this, I hope we have met our challenge in the beginning. That challenge was to present to you the events in the life of an industry in which you are now living. It was designed to provide you with a road map of the progression of how we do things today in the process of asking our human capital assets to move to another location for the benefit of the employer.

For now, the journey is complete. But the road will change with each year that follows. It is critical if the journey is to continue that you become involved in the planning of the industry in the years to come. It is critical that we find a way to return to the value-added environment that this industry was founded on.

I thank you for joining me on this journey. Despite over twenty-five years experience in the relocation industry, the journey taught me things I did not know. I hope that, likewise, it has been beneficial to you in understanding where we have been and where we are going.

Bibliography

Part One

"A Look at the Telecommunications Industry: The Baby Bells." Gil Brown. H & R Block Supplement. June 23,2004. http://www.hedgehog.com/sub/babybells.html

"A Nation of Strangers." Amazon Review. Amazon Books. March 24,2004. http://www.amazon.com/exec/obidos/tg/detail/-/067950351X/qid=1080153411/sr=1-3/ref=sr_1_3/103-6518426-0122211?v=glance&s=books

"About Fannie Mae." Federal National Mortgage Association. April 7,2004. www.fanniemae.com

"Annual Geographical Mobility Rates." U.S. Census Bureau. 2003. United States Government 23 November 2003. http://www.census.gov/population/socdemo/migration/tab-a-1.txt

Calver, Judith. "Company Practices in Employee Transfers and Relocation." New York: American Management Association. 1954.

"Company Payment of Employees' Moving Expenses." Highlights for the Executive Studies in Personnel Policy, No. 154. National Conference Board. New York: National Conference Board.

Editors. "20th Year Relocation TimeLine." Mobility Magazine. May 2000

Employee Relocation Council. Homesale Program Terminology. Washington, D.C. Employee Relocation Council. 1989.

Fradkin, Philip L. Stagecoach: Wells Fargo and the American West. New York: Simon and Schuster, 2002

Friedman, Thomas L. Lexus and the Olive Tree. New York: Anchor Books,2000. Specifically pages 80,81,133.

Glasser, William M.D., <u>Choice Theory: A New Psychology of Personal Freedom.</u> New York: Harper Collins, 1998.

Gorlin, Harriet. *Personnel Practices II: Hours of Work, pay practices, relocation.* Conference Board

"H. Cris Collie Reaches 25-year Milestone with ERC." Mobility Magazine May 1997

Holloman, Jerry. "HFS Agrees to Acquire PHH" Mobility Magazine January 1997

Kinley, John. "Company-Paid Moving Expenses for Individual Employees." Highlights for the Executive Canadian Studies, No.3. Montreal: National Industrial Conference Board, Inc. of Canada.

"Labor Force Statistics from Current Population Survey." Bureau of Labor Statistics, 2003. United States Department of Labor. 20 November 2003. http://data.bls.gov/servlet/SurveyOutputServlet

Lancaster, Lynne and David Stillman. <u>When Generations Collide</u>. New York: HarperCollins Publishers, 2002.

Lewis, Bob Karen Berman and John Featherston. "The History of the Home Purchase Service Industry" National Relocation and Real Estate. 1992.

"Loneliness." Probe Ministries. March 24,2004. http://www.probe.org/docs/lonely.html

Niskanen, William A., "Reaganomics". *The Concise Encyclopedia of Economics.* Library of Economics and Liberty. Retrieved April 19, 2004 from the World Wide Web: http://www.econlib.org/library/Enc/Reaganomics.html

Niskanen, William A. "Policy Analysis" Cato Policy Analysis No 261. October 22, 1996. Website viewed April 30,2004. http://www.cato.org/pubs/pas/pa-261.html

"Our History." Government National Mortgage Association. April 7,2004. www.ginniemae.gov/about/Our_History.asp?Section=About

" The Reagan Presidency." University of Texas. April 30,2004. http://www.reagan.utexas.edu/ref/rrpres.htm

"Reaganomics" Wikipedia. April 19,2004. http://en.wikipedia.org/wiki/Reagonomics

"Real Estate And Other Assistance for Relocated Employees." Supplement to Company Payment of Employee's Moving Expenses Studies in Personnel Policy No. 154. National Conference Board. New York: National Conference Board.

Research Catalog. Lippincott Library Catalog. University of Pennsylvania. University of Pennsylvania On-Line Catalog. http://franklinlibrary.upenn.edu

"Revenue Ruling 54-429." Internal Revenue Service. TaxLinks.com. http://www.taxlinks.com/rulings/1954/revrul54%2D429.htm

"Revenue Ruling 55-140." Internal Revenue Service. Tax Links.com. http://www.taxlinks.com/rul;ings/1955/revrul55%2D140.htm

"Revenue Ruling 59-236." Internal Revenue Service. TaxLinks.com. http://www.taxlinks.com/rulings/1959/revrul59%2D236.htm

"Revenue Ruling 59-410." Internal Revenue Service. Tax Links.com. http://www.taxlinks.com/rulings/1959/revrul59%2D410.htm

"Revenue Ruling 63-77." Internal Revenue Service. TaxLinks.com. http://www.taxlinks.com/rulings/1963/revrul63-77.htm

"Revenue Ruling 64-153." Internal Revenue Service. TaxLinks.com. http://www.taxlinks.com/rulings/1964/revrul64-153.htm

"Revenue Ruling 65-158." Internal Revenue Service. TaxLinks.com. http://www.taxlinks.com/rulings/1965/revrul65-158.htm

"Revenue Ruling 66-41." Internal Revenue Service. TaxLinks.com.

http://www. Taxlinks.com/rulings/1966/ revrul66-41.htm

"Revenue Ruling 67-48." Internal Revenue Service. TaxLinks.com. http://www.taxlinks.com/rulings/1967/revrul67-48.htm

"Tax Reform Act of 1986." Prentice Hall. April 19,2004. http://cwx.prenhall.com/bookbind/pubbooks/dye4/medialib/docs/tax1986.htm

Tax Reform Act of 1986." Free Dictionary. April 19,2004. http://encyclopedia.the free dictionary.com/Tax%20Reform%20Act%20°f%201986

"Tax Reform Act of 1986." Trading Glossary. April 20.2004. http://www.trading-glossary.com/t0077.ªsp

"Tax Reform Act of 1986." GNU Free Document. May 28,2004. http://www.worldhistory.com/wiki/T/Tax-Reform-Act-of-1986.htm

"Tax Reform Act of 1986." Ishipress. May 28,2004. http://www.ishipress.com/86reform.htm

"Tax Reform Act of 1986." Workforce Security. May 28,2004. http://www.workforcesecurity.doleta.gov/dmstree/uipi/uip187/uip/ 1287.htm

"Urea Formaldehyde Foam Insulation" US Inspect. June 26,2004. http://www.usinspect.com/UFFI/UFFI.asp

"Urea-Formaldehyde Foam Insulation (UFFI). Canada Mortgage and Housing Corporation.

June 26,2004. http://www.cmhc-schl.gc.ca/en/burema/gesein/abhose ceo6.cfm

"Who We Are" Federal National Mortgage Association. April 7,2004. http://www.freddiemac.com

Wilson, Christine. "Born of Corporate America's Need." Mobility Magazine October 1992

Wilson, Christine. "Evolution of the Relocation Management Company." November 1992

Part Two

Employee Relocation Council. <u>The Primer: A Guide to Employee Relocation and Relocation Policy Development.</u> Washington, D.C.: Employee Relocation Council. 1993.

Hall Institute of Real Estate. <u>Managing a Real Estate Team.</u> Hinsdale, IL: Dryden Press. 1980.

Needham, Terry. <u>Winning and Keeping Relocation Business.</u> Kansas City, Missouri: Relocation/Realty Consultants. 1989

Part Three

Bloom, Daniel. "A Guide to Home Purchase Programs within the Relocation Industry – Number Six in the Daniel Bloom & Associates, Inc. White Paper Series." 2002

Boschee, M.A., & Jacobs, G. (1997) "Childcare in the United States: Yesterday and Today". <u>http://www.nncc.org</u>. February 27, 2005.

Herring, Laura and Peggy Greenwood. "40 years of Corporate Relocation Policy." Mobility Magazine, August 2002.

Part Four

Bloom, Daniel. "The Relocation Process: A New Perspective on the Management of the Supply Chain" – Number Four in the Daniel Bloom & Associates, Inc. White Paper Series." 2001

Bloom, Daniel. "Where Have All The Elders Gone?" Mobility Magazine, August 2002

"Definition for Dilemma". February 13, 2005. http://www.dictionary.com

Dettmer, H. William. Goldratt's Theory of Constraints. Milwaukee: ASQ Quality Press. 1997

Fitz-Enz, Jac. The ROI of Human Capital. New York: AMACOM Books. 2000

Goldratt, Eliyahu. The Goal Second Revised Edition. Croton, NY: North River Press. 1992

Goldratt, Eliyahu. It's Not Luck. Great Barrington, MA: North River Press. 1994

Goldratt, Eliyahu. Critical Chain. Great Barrington, MA: North River Press. 1997

Goldratt, Eliyahu. Necessary But Not Sufficient. Great Barrington, MA: North River Press. 2000.

Grossman, Robert J. "The Truth About the Coming Labor Shortage" HR Magazine. March 2005. Page 46-53.

Mathis, Robert L., John H. Jackson. Human Resource Management 7th Edition. Minneapolis, MN: West Publishing Coporation.1991.

Newbold, Robert. Project Management in the Fast Lane. Boca Raton, FL: The St. Lucie Press 1998

Rackham, Neil and John R. DeVincentis. Rethinking the Sales Force: Redefining Selling to Create and Capture Customer Value. New York: McGraw-Hill. 1999.

BIBLIOGRAPHY

Worldwide ERC®. <u>Relocation Law Manual.</u> Washington, D.C.:
Worldwide ERC®, 1995

Appendices

Appendix 1

Geneology of an Industry

Since the beginning of the relocation industry there have been a number of relocation management companies which have come and gone. Below is the genealogy of the industry showing what has happened to the many companies involved in the industry over time.

1943

Interstate Relocation

1950

1951

1952

1ˢᵗ Tennessee National Bank

1953

1954

1955

Homerica ⇨ Homequity ⇨ PHH ⇨ Cendant

1956

1957

1958

1959

1960

1961

1962

EDS

Homequity ⇨ PHH ⇨ Cendant

1963

1964

Potere ⇨ Howard Relocation ⇨ Associates Relocation ⇨ Citicapital Relocation ⇨ Prudential

Royal Trust ⇨ Merged with AE LePage to form Royal LePage

1965

Executrans ⇨ Coldwell Banker ⇨ HFS ⇨ Cendant

Executive Home Counseling ⇨ Relocation Consultants ⇨ReloAction

1966

Transamerica ⇨ Homequity ⇨ PHH ⇨ Cendant

FC Tucker ⇨ No longer in buy-out business, still running residential real estate brokerage

Bank of St Louis - > GenRel Relocation ⇨ Boatmen's Relocation ⇨ Executive Relocation

Gruetzmacher Relocation ⇨ Out of Business

Republic Bank of Dallas ⇨ Associates Relocation ⇨ Citicapital Relocation ⇨ Prudential

B.F. Chamberlain Management ⇨ Executive Relocation

Van Relco ⇨ Intergroup Asset Mgt ⇨ Associates ⇨ Citicapital ⇨ Prudential

Gribin Von-Dyl ⇨ Out of Business

Sherwood & Roberts ⇨ Out of Business

Byron Reed ⇨ Transequity

Bank of Oklahoma ⇨ Out of Business

Wisconsin Transaction ⇨ Federated Relocation ⇨ Out of Business

1967

Canada Trust ⇨ Royal Le Page

Commonwealth Relocation ⇨ Transamerica Title⇨ Lawyers Title ⇨ Weichert Relocation

1968

Employee Transfer ⇨ Equitable ⇨ Travelers ⇨ Genesis ⇨ Homequity ⇨ HFS ⇨ Cendant

TI Home Transfer ⇨TICOR Relocation ⇨ Merrill Lynch Relocation ⇨ Prudential Relocation

National Residence Service ⇨ Out of Business

1969

Weichert Relocation

Executive Home Consultants ⇨ Plus Relocation

1970

Equitable ⇨ Travelers ⇨ Genesis ⇨ Homequity ⇨ PHH ⇨ HFS⇨ Cendant

Relocation Realty Service Corp ⇨ Empire of America ⇨ Coldwell Banker ⇨ HFS ⇨ Cendant

1971

Texas Commerce Bank ⇨ Associates Relocation ⇨ Citicapital Relocation ⇨ Prudential

Real Estate Plus ⇨ Plus Relocation

1972

1973

Ticor Relocation ⇨ Merrill Lynch Relocation ⇨ Prudential Relocation

1974

Schlott Realtors ⇨ Relocation 1 ⇨ Morrell and Associates ⇨ GMAC Relocation

1975

Maenner Relocation ⇨ Premier Relocation ⇨ Pinnacle Relocation ⇨ Primacy Relocation

A.E. Le Page ⇨ Merged with Royal Trust to form Royal LePage

1st National Bank of Bartlesville ⇨ Out of Business

Relocation Consultants

1976

Lutz Relocation ⇨ Home Purchase Corp ⇨ Associates ⇨ Citicapital ⇨ Prudential

1977

Better Homes and Gardens ⇨ Homequity ⇨ PHH ⇨ HFS ⇨ Cendant

1978

Relocation Resources ⇨ Weicheert Relocation

Black Horse Relocation

1979

1980

Moran, Stahl and Boyer ⇨ Merrill Lynch Relocation ⇨ Prudential

ERS Ltd ⇨ Homequity Canada ⇨ HFS ⇨ Cendant

Real Estate 1 ⇨ Relocation America

1981

ChemExecReloSystems ⇨ Associates Relocation ⇨ Citicapital Relocation ⇨ Prudential

Corporate Transfer Service ⇨ Cooperative Resource Services ⇨ SIRVA

The Relocation Group

Carolina Relocation

First National Bank of Maryland ⇨ Glaesser and Associates ⇨ Out of Business

MSI

Homepool ⇨ Cooperative Resource Services ⇨ SIRVA

1982

Pacific Relocation ⇨ ReloAction

Western Relocation ⇨ Century 21 ⇨ HFS ⇨ Cendant

Plus Relocation

Corporate Homes of America ⇨ GMAC Global Relocation

City Relocation ⇨ Relocation Resources

1983

Intergroup Asset Management ⇨ Associates Relocation ⇨ Citicapital Relocation ⇨ Prudential

US West Relocation ⇨ US Relocation ⇨ Cooperative Resource Services ⇨ SIRVA

Professional Relocation Group ⇨ Household Relocation ⇨ Coldwell Banker ⇨ Cendant

Midlantic National Bank (Franklin Capital) ⇨ Out of Business

1984

Travelers Relocation ⇨ Genesis Relocation ⇨ Homequity ⇨ HFS ⇨ Cendant

Relocation America

Howard Relocation ⇨ Associates Relocation ⇨ Citicapital Relocation ⇨ Prudential

Forward Mobility ⇨ The MI Group

Relocation 1 ⇨ Morrell and Associates ⇨ GMAC Relocation

Williams Relocation

1985

Re/Max International

Associates Relocation ⇨ Citicapital Relocation ⇨ Prudential

Corporate Relocation Services

National Equity

Premier Relocation Services

1986

Weichert Relocation

National Residential

1987

Corporate Relocation Management

Relocation Experts ⇨ Starck Relocation

American Escrow and Closing

Premier Relocation ⇨ Pinnacle Relocation ⇨ Primacy Relocation

Cross Country Relocation

1988

1989

Americorp Relocation

Preferred Relocation

DJ Knight Relocation

1990

Lifeco Relocation ⇨ Out of Business

Cornerstone Relocation

Household Relocation ⇨ Coldwell Banker ⇨ Cendant

1991

US Relocation ⇨ Cooperative Resource Services ⇨ SIRVA

The Relocation Assistance Corporation

Primacy Relocation

Armstrong Relocation ⇨ Primacy Relocation

Keystone Relocation ⇨ Out of Business

1992

Relocation Dynamics ⇨ SIRVA

First Line Relocation

1993

MML Relocation ⇨ Weichert Relocation

1994

Corporate Relocation Services (VA)

Universal Relocation ⇨ Primacy Relocation

1995

Feasibility Group ⇨ Out of business

1996

Argonaut Relocation ⇨ GMAC Relocation

1997

Resource Referral ⇨ OneSource Relocation

Paragon Decision Resources

TransferEEZ ⇨ Graebel Relocation

1998

Merdian Mobility Resources ⇨ SIRVA

1999

Access Relocation ⇨ Newport Mobility

2000

2001

2002

Lexicon Relocation

SIRVA

Graebel Relocation

Appendix 2

Geneology of the Referral Industry

Over the past forty years there have been a number of both formal and informal networks created to provide a method of passing business between real estate brokers across the country. Below is a list of the major networks that have existed within the industry.

1925

United National Real Estate ⇨ United Country Real Estate

1950

1951

1952

1953

1954

1955

Homerica

1956

1957

1958

1959

1960

American Family Relocation ⇨ Out of Business

RELO

All Points ⇨ RELO

Gallery of Homes ⇨ First referral network⇨ out of business

1961

National Multi-List Service ⇨ Home for Living

1962

1963

1964

1965

1966

1967

1968

1969

1970

1971

ICR ⇨ Equinet ⇨ Travelers Realty Network ⇨ Genesis Relocation ⇨ RELO

1972

ERA Franchise System

1973

Re/Max

1974

1975

1976

INRELCO

1977

Red Carpet

1978

1979

TRANSLO ⇨ Associates ⇨ RELO

Family Relocation Service (BH&G)

1980

VIP Referral Network (Century 21)

Relocation 200

1980

Refnet

1981

Midwesco Relocation Services

1982

1983

1984

Equinet ⇨ Travelers ⇨ Genesis ⇨ RELO

1985

1986

1987

Amerinet ⇨ Travelers ⇨ Genesis ⇨ RELO

Travelers ⇨ Genesis ⇨ RELO

1988

Independent Brokers of America

Genesis ⇨ RELO

1989

1990

1991

Genesis Realty Network ⇨ RELO

1992

1993

1994

1995

1996

1997

Reliance Relocation Services ⇨ RELO

1998

Relocation Solutions Network ⇨ Out of business

1999

2000

2001

2002

2003

There were also a group of lesser known referral networks which have come and gone during the time span represented by our journey. Below is a list of those networks

Advantage Relocation Network

AIM 100

Alternative Relocation Network

City to City Relocation

Execusystems – Spin off of Realty Executives

Fifty-Fifty Referral

Homeowners Relocation Service

International Referral Exchange

National Home Relocation Service

National Realty Relocation Associates

National Relocation Network

National Transfer Relocation

Nationwide ⇨ Coldwell Banker

Network 50 ⇨ Merrill Lynch ⇨ Prudential

North American Brokers Association

Property Consulting Service of America

Real Estate USA (1980's)

Realex

RECOA (1970's)

Referral Center Inc.

TAREX

Transforce

United Referral Network

Appendix 3

The Founders of the Industry

Below is a list of the founders of this industry and the companies that they are associated with:

Joseph and Vincent Aveni – Corporate Relocation Management

Ted Bell - Employee Transfer Corporation

A. T. Bliss Jr. – National Residential Service

Bob Bower – ERS Ltd

Ed Carroll – Relocation Realty Service Corporation

B.F. Chamberlain – B.F. Chamberlain Management Company

Bill Decker – Carolina Relocation Group

Weston Edwards – Pioneer Title Relocation

Dick Farance – Pacific Relocation

Jim Fissell – Western Relocation

Charles Gardiner – Transamerica Title Relocation

Bob Glaeser – First National Bank of Maryland

Walter Hall - Relocation Resourcces Inc.

Eileen Halley – Relocation Group

Dan Hanrahan – Potere Relocation

Sue Haskell – US West Relocation

Carroll Hassler – Relocation Realty Service Corporation

Frank Hodges – A.E. LePage Relocation

Greg Hutchins – Intergroup Relocation

Jean Jones - Intergroup Relocation

John Kovach – Bank of St Louis

Russ LaChance – Americorp Relocation

Lloyd "Mick" Lee – Plus Relocation

Derek Lewin – Intergroup Relocation

Frank Madden – Homequity, Executrans, ChemExecRelo Systems

Jack Maenner – Maenner Relocation

Don McPherson -Homerica

Richard Montgomery – Corporate Relocation Services

Frank Patitucci – Relocation Consultants

Bill Plummer – Americorp Relocation

Mark Roussey - Re/Max Relocation

John Rowell – Relocation Group

Ray Quist – Corporate Transfer Service

Appendix 4

The Circle Unbroken

In the process of conducting our research we have found that there are a number of offspring of the founders of this industry working in the industry today:

Noreen Morrell – Daughter Kelly Reiss works for Relocation Dynamics

Meri Hill – Daughter Cathy Bullock works for Xonex Relocation

Gordon Graham – Son Todd Graham now running AE Worldwide

Paul Taylor – Son Joe Taylor works for Valuation Administrators

Sally Berning – Daughter Elizabeth is the relocation manager for Sony Electronics

Laura Herring - Daughter Lauren Herring works for The Impact Group

William Roper – Son William Roper Jr. works for Cendant Mobility

Robert Walczak – Son Bruce Walczak owns Relocation Consultants

Bruce Walkczak - Daughter Cathlin Walczak works for Cendant Mobility

Don Estrin – Son Brad works for Suddath Relocation Systems

Harvey Auger – Son Chip works for Homebanc Mortgage

Appendix 5

Relocation Research Studies

*Using the resources of the software program Endnote Version 7.0, the au-
thor researched the holdings of some of the three hundred sixty-two catalogs
of professional papers located in library catalogs around the world. Based
on the data contained therein, here is the list of the corporate relocation
related transfer studies completed during the time period covered by this
work.*

1950

1951

1952

1953

1954

American Management Association. *Corporate Practices in Employee
Transfers.*

1955

DeMott, J. M. *How Management May Convince Its Employees to Make a
Geographic Relocation.* Drexel Institute of Technology.

1956

Conference Board. *Corporate Payment of Moving Expenses.*

1957

1958

1959

Conference Board of Canada. *Corporate Paid Moving Expenses.*

1960

Marzullo, Ferdinand. *The Problems and Expense of Transferring Employees.* Wharton School Thesis in Economics.

Conference Board. *Employees on the Move.* September 1960

1961

1962

Transferred Employees with Homes to Sell. Conference Board December 1962.

1963

Home Purchase Loans for Transferred Employees. Conference Board March 1963

1964

Government Accounting Office. *Excessive Relocation Payments to Employees Transferred from One Company Location to Another.*

White, Karol. *Reimbursing Personnel for Relocation Expenses.* American Management Association.

1965

Chartier, A. E. *New Patterns in Company Paid Moving Expenses in Canada.* Conference Board of Canada.

Changes in Company Aid to Transferred Home Owners. Conference Board March 1965

1966

Conference Board. *Real Estate and Other Assistance for Relocation of Employees.*

American Management Association. *Plant Relocation: A Case History of a Move.*

1967

1968

1969

Bureau of Labor Statistics. *Plant Movement, Transfer and Relocation Allowances*

1970

Terry, William. *Relocation Expenses in Canada.* Conference Board of Canada

Marsh, R. M. *Family Disruption during the Moving Process.*

1971

1972

1973

Mann, Michael. *Workers on the Move: The Sociology of Relocation.* Cambridge Studies in Sociology. Cambridge University. Cambridge, United Kingdom.

Seidenberg, R. *Corporate Wives —Corporate casualties?* AMACOM

1974

Employee Relocation Council. *Relocation Assistance: Transferred Employees*

Employee Relocation Council. *Comprehensive Survey of Corporate Policies*

1975

Employee Relocation Council. *Relocation Assistance: Newly Hired Employees*

Employee Relocation Council. *Comprehensive Survey of International Relocation Policies*

1976

Business International Corporation. *Transferring Personnel to Difficult Locations.* BI Management Monographs No.59.

Employee Relocation Council. *International Survey of Relocation Policies*

Employee Relocation Council. *Comprehensive Survey of Relocation Policies: Current Employees.*

1977

Wong, Kenneth. *Relocation Policies and Practices in Canada.* Conference Board of Canada.

Gorlin, Harriet. *Elements of Corporate Relocation Assistance Policies.* Conference Board.

Buckley, P.J. *Multinational Firms and International Relocation.* New Horizons in International Business.

Trost, Alice. *Employment and the Urban Pool: Impact of Job Relocation.* Garland Studies in the History of American Labor.

Employee Relocation Council. *Relocation Trends Survey.*

Employee Relocation Council. *International Survey*

1978

Mark Clements Research. *Business on the Move.*

Employee Relocation Council. *Comprehensive Survey of Relocation Policies: Current Employees.*

1979

American Institute for Public Policy Research. *Restrictions on Business Mobility.*

Employee Relocation Council. *Moving Expense Reimbursements*

Employee Relocation Council. *Comprehensive Survey of International Relocation Policies*

1980

Employee Relocation Council. *The Effect of Job Transfer on Employees and Their Families*

Employee Relocation Council. *Comprehensive Survey of Relocation Policies: New Hires*

Employee Relocation Council. *Survey of Mortgagees, Housing and Cost of Living Assistance.*

Jago, A. *Employee Relocation Expenses.* Institute of Personnel Management. London.

Hagen Marketing Research. *Study of Employee Relocation Policies Among Major US Corporation.* Merrill Lynch Relocation Management.

1981

Gorlin, Harriet. *Personnel Practices II: Hours of Work, pay practices, relocation.* Conference Board

Frank, J.G. *Provincial Differences: Challenge to Compensation and Relocation Policies.* Conference Board of Canada

Atlas Van Lines. *Annual Forum on Moving.*

1982

Chartier, A.E. *Relocation in Canada: Policies and Practices.* Conference Board of Canada.

Merrill Lynch Relocation Management. *Relocation Management Quarterly.*

Fisher, Cynthia. *Transfer Transitions.* Office of Naval Research.

1983

Residential Mobility, Workplace Relocation and the Journey to Work. Ph.D. Thesis Brown University

Meidinger International Services. *International Transfers.*

Catalyst. *Human Factors in Relocation: Corporate and Employee Points of View.*

Fields, J.P., S. Erkut. *Relocation as Nemesis: A Study of Black and White Dual Career Couples.* Center for Research on Women.

Kelton, Christine M..L. *Trends in Relocation of U.S. Manufacturing.* Research in Business Economics and Public Policy. Ph.D. Thesis University of Wisconsin.

Marsh, Raymond. *Family Disruption during the Moving Process.* Thesis. Brandeis University

LaGrande, L.H. and Library of Congress. *Worker Relocation Assistance: Move People to Jobs.* Congressional Research Service.

1984

Johnson, A. A. *Relocation of two-career couples.*

1985

Conference Board. *Corporations and Families: Changing Practices and Perspectives.*

Majchrzak , Ann. AT&T Relocation Study. Western Electric Research Foundation. Purpose was to study the effect of technological change and plant relocation on unskilled and semiskilled workers.

1986

Erkut, S, J.P. Fields. *Finding Solutions to Relocation Problems of Professionals.* Center for Research on Women.

Employee Relocation Council. *White Paper on Radon Gas*

1987

Employee Relocation Council. *Relocation Trends and Developments.*

Employee Relocation Council. *Impact of the Changing Family on Employee Relocation.*

Employee Relocation Council. *International Experience Index.*

Allied Van Lines. *Mobility Trends.*

Atlas Van Lines. *Annual Survey of Corporate Moving Practices.*

Shortland, Susan. *Managing Relocation.* Industrial Relations in Practice.

Zak, J.S. *Quits, Moves, Spatial Equilibrium, and Workplace Relocation.* National Bureau of Economic Research.

James, Syme. *Adjustment to office Relocations: Information Received, Employee Status and Ease of Adjustment.* M.S. Thesis Cornell University.

1988

Employee Relocation Council. *Relocation Trends and Developments.*

Bureau of National Affairs. *Employee Relocation Programs: Help for Two Paycheck Households.*

Atlas Van Lines. *Annual Survey of Corporate Relocation Policies.*

Allied Van Lines. *Innovations in Relocation Management.*

Borg, Malcolm. *International Transfers of Managers in Multi-National Corporations.* Ph.D. Thesis, Uppsala University.

Lang. Denise. *Phantom Spouse: Helping You and Your Family Survive Business Travel or Relocation*

1989

Employee Relocation Council. *Relocation Trends and Developments.*

Employee Relocation Council. *Relocation Assistance: Transferred Employees*

Employee Relocation Council. *Relocation Trends Survey*

Residence Inn by Marriott. *Employees on the Move: The Impact of Relocation.*

1990

Employee Relocation Council. *Relocation Trends Survey*

Employee Relocation Council. *Impact of Societal Shifts and Corporate Changes on Corporate Relocation.*

Residence Inn by Marriott. *Home on the Road.*

Hendershott, Anne B. *Moving for Work: The Sociology of Relocation in the 1990's.*

Johnson, Arlene. *Relocation of the Two-Earner Couples: What Companies are Doing.* Conference Board.

Lang. Denise. *Phantom Spouse: Helping You and Your Family Survive Business Travel or Relocation*

McCollum, A.T. *Trauma of Moving: Psychological Issues for Women. .* Sage Library of Social Responsibility

BTA Economic Research Institute. *Geographic Entry-level Salary Survey and Relocation Reference*

1991

Employee Relocation Council. *Relocation Assistance: Newly Hired Employees.*

Employee Relocation Council. *Relocation Trends Survey*

Pont. Daniel A.: *Stress and Satisfaction Following Relocation.* M.S. Thesis, Colorado State University.

Zak, J.J. *Moving to the Suburbs: Do Relocating Companies Leave their Black Employees Behind*. Harvard Institute of Economic Research.

Honeychurch, R.R. and H.K. Battler. *Complete Relocation Kit: Everything You Need to Know About Changing Homes, Jobs and Communities.* Dearborn Financial.

1992

Employee Relocation Council. *Relocation Trends Survey.*

Employee Relocation Council. *Relocation Assistance: Transferred Employees*

Munton, A.G. *Managing People on the Move.*

Coyle, Wendy. *International Relocation: A Global Perspective.* Management Today.

1993

Employee Relocation Council. *Relocation Trends Survey*

Employee Relocation Council. *International Survey*

Munton, A. G. *Job Relocation: Managing People on the Move.* John Wiley

Pencak, Christine. *An Investigation into Personal and Situational Determinants of the Willingness to Relocate.* PhD, Thesis. Wayne State University.

1994

Employee Relocation Council. *Relocation Trends Survey*

1995

Employee Relocation Council. *Relocation Trends Survey.*

Employee Relocation Council. *Relocation Assistance: Transferred Employees.*

Runzheimer International. *Survey and Analysis of Employee Relocation Policies and Costs.*

Kennedy, David. *On the Move: A Case Study of Management Relocation in the Lodging Industry.* Masters in Professional Studies Thesis. Cornell University.

Hendershott, Ann. *Moving For Work: Sociology of Relocation in the 1990's.* University of America.

Papalia, Anthony. *An Inside Look at Outplacement Counseling: Relocation of Smith –Corona to Mexico.*

Sohn, Ned. *Cost Management Redbook for Employee Relocation Homesale Real Estate Transactions.*

Right Associates. *Valuing Dual Career Workforce.* University of Tennessee at Chattanooga.

1996

Rogers, Susan Burns. *Military Wives and Attachment Theory: A Correlational Study of Frequent Family Relocations and Attachment Theory.* Amherst College Thesis.

Burger, Bettina. *Impact of Corporate Moving :Real Trends of the Real Estate Broker.* University of Southern California. Research Institute for Business and Economics.

Employee Relocation Council. *New Hire Survey.*

Employee Relocation Council. *Issues in Relocation.*

Lewis, S. and J. Lewis. *The work-Family Challenge: Rethinking Employment.* Sage Publications

Tickell, Adam and D. Coates. *Relocation within the European Union* .European Parliament.

U.S. Census Bureau. *Recent Movers.*

1997

Employee Relocation Council. *International Relocation Issues Report*

Marshall, Alan. *Generation X Relocation Guide.* AOP Books.

Trost, A.E. *Employment and Urban Poor:Impact of Job Relocations.* Garland Studies in the History of American Labor.

1998

Employee Relocation Council. *Relocation Assistance: Transferred Employees.*

Employee Relocation Council. *Family Issues*

Employee Relocation Council. *Relocation Tax Issues.*

Jensen, Anita K. *International Relocation: A Family Perspective.* Ph.D. Thesis. Fielding Institute. University of Michigan.

Baker & McKenzie. *International Executive Transfer Update.*

1999

Employee Relocation Council. *Current Issues in Relocation.*

Windham International. *Global Relocation Trends.*

Kennedy, David. *On the Road Again: An Investigation of Situational and Intentional Antecedents of Job Relocation Decisions in the Service Sector.* Ph.D. Thesis. Cornell University.

2000

United States. Office of Management and Budget. *Information on Relocation Expenses for Federal Employees.*

Ommeren, Jos Van. *Commuting and Relocation Jobs and Residences.* Aldershot.

Watson Wyatt Worldwide. *Exhibit Book of Employee Relocation Policies.*

2001

Employee Relocation Council. *Family Issues.*

Employee Relocation Council. *Relocation Assistance: Transferred Employees.*

Kennedy, David. *Job Relocation Decisions in the Service Sector: A Qualitative and Quantitative Study.* School of Industrial Relations and Organisational Behavior.

2002

Employee Relocation Council. *New Hire Survey*

Employee Relocation Council. *International Survey.*

2003

Employee Relocation Council. *Transfer Volume and Cost Survey.*

Wolf-Wendel, Lisa, S. Trombly, S. Rice. *The two-body-problem: dual-career-couple hiring policies in higher education.* John Hopkins University

2004

Employee Relocation Council. *Family Issues Report.*

2005

Employee Relocation Council . *Relocation Assistance: Transferred Executives*

Appendix 6

Samuel Carter Letter to Wells Fargo Headquarters

Below is the full text of the letter that is described on page 11 of this work, as provided by Andy Anderson. Mr. Anderson is the corporate historian for the Wells Fargo Company based in San Francisco, California.

Mr. Morgan

Dr. Sir

Below please find a copy of letter recd yesterday from Saml Carter

Yours

Wm B Rochester

"COPY"

Messrs Wells Fargo & Co   San Francisco June 30/52

Gents

Here I am at last in this fast community I arrived Sunday the 27th sick, had an attack of fever on the passage up but having the very best of attention on Shipboard began to improve before I arrived, was very feeble so much so that I was hardly able to walk, much less to write or I should have written by the Gold Gate that sailed at 7 o'clock Monday morning—On Monday I got out feeling that I <u>must</u> do so, made several calls on business men, was very cordially received, great attention shown me by all. Judge Chamber and Mr. Haight of the firm of Page Bacon & Co were very polite, gave me all the advice and information in reference to business in their power, there was not a suitable office to be had at any price in the street or vicinity. I got eye on a fine <u>fire proof</u> store (new) in just the right place, the Lessee had just got it fitted up with shelves, etc for fancy goods, only 4 doors from Adams & Co. I heard he was waiting for the goods to arrive, looked him up & after a long talk hired him to assign over his lease to me for which I gave him $1000 in <u>per month in advance</u>, an awful price I know, but it was that or nothing & I did not propose to be bluffed off, do not be frightened at my seeming extravagance, good business men here say I got a good hit, in fact I can sell out today and make money even on the bonus I paid. You must not have any conscience in making & collecting charges on Cal frt & pkgs, anything I want I am obliged to pay at least 400 prct. Over N.Y. prices. Carpenters chg $8.00 per day for labor in fitting up office - $7.50 for an office chair in N.Y. 12/ - other things in proportion. Col McK thought I had got high notions about expenses here -- $25 per week is the best I can do for board, unless I room myself & eat at the saloons then they chg $14 per week for breakfast and dinner - washing $3.00 per doz, 2/ for cigars, 2/ for blacking

---

boots, 8/ for cutting hair.

Adams & Co are drawing at 3% & how they manage to make any-thing out of that I cannot tell if they pay 2% frt & insurance – I met FM Hubbard, here, formerly of Buffalo – he is well posted up, has spent most of the time with me – also Mr. Rochesters brother, Hubbard has been all through the mines & up to Oregon & I should judge favorably known as soon as I feel able shall go up the country after getting the office well underway fitting up.

Adams & Co do not stand well here among the Bankers from what I can learn, they attempt to be very smart in many of their operations, I have had many good promises for patronage as soon as I can get a going – am in hopes to be able to make shipment on the 15th of July but can't tell how large yet, must begin to do something soon or I shall ruin the Co you will think and have good occasion for thinking so I fear, but bear in mind this is California & if we can only get a chance to make some charges for do-ing business that will balance off for those I have to pay, I think some of them will sweat. If my health was only good I should feel in good spirits, I am improving & they all tell me I will soon get strength & flesh – I am 21 lbs lighter than when I left N.Y. think I shall be right in a few days. I have not been about the City only in the vicinity of Montgomery St. the Wall St. of San Francisco & of course cannot say what I think of it but from what I have seen must say there is much more of a real legitimate business appearance than I had anticipated.

Printed in the United States
29372LVS00002B/223-282

9 781932 966343